TRUE COUNT
TO
PENTECOST

TRUE COUNT TO PENTECOST

Brother Arnold Bowen

XULON PRESS

Xulon Press
2301 Lucien Way #415
Maitland, FL 32751
407.339.4217
www.xulonpress.com

© 2021 by Brother Arnold Bowen

All rights reserved solely by the author. The author guarantees all contents are original and do not infringe upon the legal rights of any other person or work. No part of this book may be reproduced in any form without the permission of the author.

Due to the changing nature of the Internet, if there are any web addresses, links, or URLs included in this manuscript, these may have been altered and may no longer be accessible. The views and opinions shared in this book belong solely to the author and do not necessarily reflect those of the publisher. The publisher therefore disclaims responsibility for the views or opinions expressed within the work.

Unless otherwise indicated, Scripture quotations taken from the King James Version (KJV) – *public domain*.

Paperback ISBN-13: 978-1-66282-636-8
Ebook ISBN-13: 978-1-66282-637-5

Table of Contents

Chapter 1 Examining Leviticus 23:16 1

Chapter 2 PAUL and THOUSANDS KEEPING PENTECOST 9

Chapter 3 Acts 1:5 31

Chapter 4 The Hebrew Word for unto/ until in Leviticus 23:16 is "ad" . . . 51

Chapter 5 Which Of the Two Wheat Harvests (That Are in the World Today) Is The Scriptural Pentecost Wheat Harvest of old??? 55

Chapter 6 Punctuation marks 61

Chapter 7 Aaron and Pentecost 69

Chapter 8 Law Given on Pentecost 71

Chapter 9 The Prophet Joel's Pentecost 75

Chapter 10 NUMBERING 79

Chapter 11 Day Another argument 97

Chapter 12 THE COUNT 103

Chapter 13 Journey to the Mount
and Count and Number 107

Chapter 14 Days Travelling to the Mount ... 125

Chapter 15 The Prophet Ezra............. 131

Chapter 16 WHAT ABOUT JOSEPHUS?... 157

Chapter 1

Examining Leviticus 23:16

Pentecost is one of the three commanded feasts of YHWH, the first fruits of the wheat harvest, and it commemorates the giving of the law at Mount Sinai.

Pentecost is the only one of the three feasts that we have to count for, the other two are on fixed days on the 15th of the first and seventh months.

True Pentecost is Observed after numbering 50 days AFTER the Seventh Sabbath is counted, instead of the traditional 50 Days after the Wave Sheaf, according to Leviticus 23:16, and this is one truth I want to share.

Lamentation 2:6 says, "I will cause them to forget my Sabbath's and feast days, and Daniel 7:25 says they will think to change times/appointments and laws, and that God would allow it for a certain period of time, which that time is up.

This book will show that the time is up for not knowing when the true Sabbaths and Feast days are, including Pentecost.

One example I give shows where the apostle Paul and thousands of believing Jews/Israelites were observing Pentecost BEYOND the traditional 50-day count, which kills the traditional 50-day count!

Leviticus 23:16 is understood two different ways, but only one is correct.

The famous Sherlock Holmes, by Sir Arthur Conan Doyle, was famous for saying **"when the impossible has been removed, whatever remains, however improbably, must be the truth"**.

Again, this book will conclusively prove that it is **Scripturally**, **Mathematically**, **Scientifically**, and even **Agriculturally IMPOSSIBLE** for Leviticus 23:16 to be understood as counting 50 days after the wave sheaf, as the traditional Pentecost keepers do, and when that **IMPOSSIBILITY** is removed what remains is numbering 50 days **AFTER** THE SEVENTH SABBATH.

Leviticus 23:16 says, "even unto the morrow "AFTER" the SEVENTH SABBATH shall you number 50 days and ye shall offer a new meat/grain offering to YHWH".

Again, the traditional third month Pentecost, is 50 days after the wave sheaf, and not 50 days after the seventh Sabbath, making it **Scripturally**, **Mathematically**, **Scientifically,** and even **Agriculturally IMPOSSIBLE, as we will see!**

Nature and mathematical certainties do not lie, therefore what remains is the true Pentecost.

We will start with **Leviticus 23:16** and see what the command says, and doesn't say, and then how the command was interpreted and carried out, by the children of Israel. It says, "even unto the morrow "AFTER" the SEVENTH SABBATH shall you number 50 days and ye shall offer a new meat/grain offering to YHWH".

Notice it clearly says the morrow AFTER the seventh Sabbath shall ye number the 50 days, it does not say to number 50 days after the wave sheaf, and then offer the new meat offering, but 50 days "after" the "Seventh Sabbath"!

Notice also the seven Sabbaths are COUNTED but the 50 days are NUMBERED which I will deal with in another chapter. The 50 days are "numbered" AFTER the seven Sabbaths are "counted" and "**THEN**" the new meat or grain offering is offered.

You must FIRST count seven Sabbaths complete and THEN number 50 days AND THEN bring a new grain offering.

It is the seven Sabbaths that are complete up "until" the Morrow after the seventh Sabbath, which according to the traditional count is 49 days NOT 50 days! Please read the verse again!

Notice also, the verse does not say to number ONE day AFTER the seven Sabbaths are counted and then bring it, but number 50 days AFTER the seventh Sabbath and then bring it. Remember Pentecost means 50 NOT one i.e., Number 50 days after the seventh Sabbaths, not 1 day, and then bring the new grain offering.

I understand how someone could think this verse could be understood differently and that is strictly because of tradition, but it is not founded in Scripture because there is no example or anything in Scripture to support this understanding.

We will examine the Scriptures in this book and see how Moses and the ancient Israelites understood it, and then we will have the truth on the matter, because they were eyewitnesses and actually lived it.

We will examine another one of the impossibilities of a traditional third month Pentecost which involves the second chapter of Joel 2:24 – 32 where YHWH Himself says that the floors would be full of WHEAT and the WINE PRESSES full of WINE/GRAPES, referring to Pentecost, and He does not lie. This prophecy came to pass on the day of Pentecost in Acts

2:15 – 17, where they were being accused of being drunk on the New Wine.

Acts 2:15-17 KJV says,
[15] For these are not drunken, as ye suppose, seeing it is but the third hour of the day. [16] **But this is "that which was spoken by the prophet Joel"**; (Remember Joel said that the wine presses would be full of wine) [17] And it shall come to pass in the last days, saith God, I will pour out of my Spirit upon all flesh: and your sons and your daughters shall prophesy, and your young men shall see visions, and your old men shall dream dreams:"

The thing about this is that it is AGRICULTURALLY IMPOSSIBLE to have the New Wine and the wine presses being full in the third month, for the traditional third month Pentecost, nature does not lie either, and will not allow it, because the GRAPES are not even ripe at that time, but the early grapes harvest will be ripe in the fourth month, for Pentecost 50 days after the seventh sabbaths are numbered, fulfilling the prophecy, then they could be accused of being drunk with the new wine from the wine presses!

This alone kills the traditional Pentecost count.

The same is true when they came into the land and were commanded to reap the harvest thereof/barley then count seven Sabbaths complete and then number the 50 days. There would be no grapes ripe for the wine presses unless you number 50 days "after" the seventh Sabbaths are counted instead of numbering 50 days after the wave sheaf. **This alone should make people take another look at their traditional third month Pentecost because YHWH did not lie through the prophet Joel.**

Joel's prophecy was fulfilled on the day of Pentecost in Acts 2:16 where they were being accused of being drunk with the NEW WINE from the wine presses that Joel's prophecy spoke of.

How could the day of Pentecost have been in the third month when it is agriculturally **IMPOSSIBLE** to have wine in the presses as the prophet Joel prophesied, when the GRAPES are not yet ripe in the third month???

Not only does Nature itself disprove the traditional third month Pentecost but I will also show that the traditional Pentecost is also MATHEMATICALLY IMPOSSIBLE.

Again, I will show eyewitnesses from Scripture how the apostle Paul and many thousands of believing Israelite were keeping Pentecost "beyond" the traditional 50-day count after the wave sheaf, and much more, but before I do, I will continue to deal extensively with **Leviticus 23:16** and show how ancient Israelites understood it.

Chapter 2

PAUL and THOUSANDS KEEPING PENTECOST BEYOND the TRADITIONAL PENTECOST!

DID YOU KNOW IT IS A MATHEMATICAL CERTAINTY THAT APOSTLE PAUL AND THOUSANDS OF BELIEVING JEWS KEPT PENTECOST "BEYOND" THE TRADITIONAL 50 DAY COUNT???

Most people know that with the traditional Pentecost you only have 50 days from the morrow after the Sabbath or wave sheaf at Passover to Pentecost but WHAT MOST DO NOT KNOW is that Paul and company left Philippi headed to Jerusalem for Pentecost at after the days of Unleavened Bread, **Acts 20:6,** intending to keep Pentecost in Jerusalem which is **1000 miles away**, according to the map in the back of most Bibles, and **the Scripture teaches they only had 8 "travel days" to make the 1000 mile journey " the traditional Pentecost"!**

You might ask **why only 8 days and not 50 days???**

Notice I said **TRAVEL** days and with the traditional 50 days to Pentecost there is only **8 TRAVEL DAYS** because we can account for **AT LEAST 42 of the 50 days to Pentecost** that they were **NOT TRAVELING** in Paul's journey from Philippi to Jerusalem for Pentecost according to **Acts 20:6 through 24:12** which I will show in a minute. Now with the true Pentecost that is 50 days AFTER the 7th Sabbath instead of 50 days after the wave sheaf or traditional Sabbath that falls within the days of Unleavened Bread, Leviticus 23:16, you would have an **additional 50 days to make the 1000-mile journey**. It is absolutely IMPOSSIBLE for them to have made it in **8 days** which automatically kills the traditional Pentecost doctrine.

How do we know they did not travel 50 straight days???

Because Scripture teaches a running count from Philippi to Jerusalem beginning in Acts 20:6 where they abode in Troas for 7 DAYS etc., days where they were **NOT TRAVELING** during the traditional 50 days to Pentecost count.

Acts 21:4 also records ANOTHER 7 DAY STAY in which they were NOT TRAVELING during the 50 day count etc., which I will explain so that anyone can see that after adding all the other NO TRAVEL days with these 14 days, it will **total 42 NO TRAVEL** days leaving **only 8 Travel Days in which to make the 1000-mile journey which was an impossibility in those days because of limited means of travel.**

The Scripture teaches that they did not travel nonstop straight through to Jerusalem but had many layovers during the traditional 50-day count and the 50-day clock was still ticking during these layovers.

If we can scripturally prove the above, it should end the Pentecost debate once and for all because you have thousands of eyewitnesses in Scripture of people keeping Pentecost **BEYOND** the traditional 50-day count.

The following conclusively shows after narrowing things down that the Apostle Paul and company only had 8 TRAVELING DAYS to travel 1000 mi. in order to keep the traditional Pentecost at Jerusalem. Again, this makes the traditional Pentecost an impossibility.

This also kills the traditional Sabbath keeping, see my booklet on Proof That the True Weekly Sabbaths Are Determined by the Phases of the Moon. http://lunarsabbath.info/index.html

If Paul only had 8 travel days in which to travel 1000 mi., this would be an average of 125 mi. per day and about 100 of these miles were on foot, half of which, with animals and an old disciple from Caesarea to Jerusalem. (They would have another 50 days to make the journey, numbering 50 days after the seventh Sabbath.)

According to the map in my Bible it is about 150 mi. from Philippi to Troas and it took them **five** of the 8 travel days by ship to travel it according to Scripture,

Acts 20:6, which is an average of 30 mi. per day. After this, the Scripture shows about 7 more examples where they were still only averaging about 30 mi. per day for the 1st 500 mi. according to my map and Scripture.

This can be verified by reading Acts 20:13 through 17 and measuring the distance between these cities with the map in the back of most Bibles, and comparing the days with the miles.

This gives us a scriptural precedence of how many miles they average per day by ship, which was the fastest means of travel of that day. On foot, a small number of men could average 15 or 20 miles per day which is verified by Scripture, bible scholars and commentators.

Again, the above statement about the 8 travel days and the 1000 mi. can be proven, which I will do shortly, this makes the traditional Pentecost impossible leaving only the true Pentecost count which is 50 days after the 7th Sabbath instead of 50 days after the wave sheaf or Sabbath that falls within the days of Unleavened Bread.

True Count to Pentecost

Please consider the following. The map shows that it is 150 miles from Philippi to Troas and the Scripture shows that it took them five of the 8 travel days to make the 150-mile journey, Acts 20:6, this leaves only "3" travel days to travel the other 850 miles to Jerusalem!

This means they would have to average over 283 miles per day. And as I said above, some of these miles would be on foot, with women and children, and herding animals, etc.

Did Paul and company average 283 1/3 miles per day or 850 mi. in 3days? Absolutely not. They only averaged about 30 mi. per day for the 1st 500 mi. according to Scripture and this should make the honest truth seeker take another look at Leviticus 23:16 and number the 50 days AFTER the 7th Sabbath instead of the wave sheaf, and that would give them another 50 days in order to have enough time to reach Jerusalem and keep the Pentecost that Paul and the thousands of Jews were keeping in the book of Acts.

If they used 2 more of the remaining 3 travel days in order to go another 60 mi., this would leave another

790 mi. and only 1 day to travel it. They did not have jet planes.

The reason Paul only had 8 travel days with the traditional count is because the Scripture records at least 42 days BEFORE Pentecost that there was "**no travel days**" for the Apostle and company, and this is not even counting some of the 7 weekly Sabbaths that would have also fallen during the 50 days. When we subtract 42 from 50 it leaves only "8 travel days" to make the 1000 mi. journey.

Here's how I scripturally come up with 42 no travel days during the traditional 50-day count to Pentecost. I will also show how that Paul had arrived at Jerusalem at least 10 days before Pentecost but 1st let's start at Philippi and pinpoint the days that they were not traveling during the traditional 50-day count to Pentecost.

Of course they were not traveling when the 50 day count began during the 7 days of Unleavened Bread at Philippi and for those that begin the 50 day count to Pentecost from the wave sheaf on the 16th of the 1st month, this would account for at least **six** of the **no**

travel days, assuming they left the very next day after Unleavened Bread.

The Scripture says they sailed away from Philippi AFTER the days of Unleavened Bread and came unto them in Troas in FIVE DAYS, where they abode 7 DAYS, Acts 20:6. This 7 day stay would account for another 7 days that they were not traveling but the traditional 50 day count is still clicking on. This is a total of 13 NO TRAVEL DAYS during the traditional 50-day count. When you subtract 13 from 50 it leaves 37 travel days to travel the rest of the distance.

Paul sailed by Ephesus to Miletus and sent up to Ephesus for the elders to come down to Miletus and if he immediately sent a runner, it would have taken at least 3DAYS to go up and find the elders and bring them back down to Miletus which is 20 miles one way. And then they had a meeting, Verse 17.

At any rate, when looking at the map, Miletus as 20 miles one way and 3days is not unreasonable when counting the trip up, notifying the elders, and then 20 miles back and then the meeting itself. This is a total of 16 days that they were NOT traveling during the traditional 50-day count.

They tarried 7 MORE DAYS at Tyre, Acts 21:4, a total of 23 NO TRAVEL DAYS. They left Tyre and abode ONE-DAY with brethren in verse 7 a total of 24 NO TRAVEL DAYS during the traditional 50-day count leaving only 26 travel days. They left the brethren and came unto Caesarea and they tarried there MANY DAYS on top of the 24 no travel days we already have, Acts 21:10. It is obvious that they made good time finding ships, weather, etc. so they were now ahead of schedule and no longer had to depend on the ship's captain and schedule, weather, etc. and they are now in charge of their own schedule because the rest of the journey is on foot and now being ahead of schedule, they decided to spend the extra time at the Evangelist's house.

I will be very generous and only count 8 NO TRAVEL DAYS at Caesarea. I'm not going to pretend that I believe it was only 8 days because we find the word "many" used by the same author of Acts and it usually would not be understood to mean less than 40.

He uses such phrases as MANY WORDS, and we would not think that this would be 8words. He uses the phrase MANY DAYS, when referring to the Messiah being seen of them "MANY DAYS" and in another place, speaking of the same event, it says, being seen of them 40 DAYS. Another place speaks of being beaten with MANY STRIPES and another place says 40 stripes save one. So, we see the phrase "many" being more equal to 40 than 8 etc., so I am being generous by only allowing 8 days instead of 40. The phrase MANY THOUSANDS is also used and when we look at the phrase many stripes, many days, and many words, and many thousands, they all refer to more than eight, therefore allowing only 8days is being very generous to say the least. Another reason to believe that "many days" would be more than 8 days is Luke, who is credited for writing the book of acts, could remember as high as 7 days twice, five days once, 3 days, 1day, etc. I feel he could have remembered 8 days and by him saying "many days" suggests it was more than 8, maybe 15 or 20, or at least enough days that he did not remember the exact number, perhaps 39 or 40 and therefore he said MANY DAYS because they were so many that he did not remember the exact number but knew it was many days.

At any rate, even with allowing as few as 8 days, this still brings us to a total of 32 NO TRAVEL days that Paul was NOT TRAVELING during the traditional 50 day count and if we stopped counting here with the traditional Pentecost count of 50 days from Unleavened Bread to Pentecost you would only have 18 TRAVEL days left in which to travel the 1000 miles to Jerusalem from Philippi which would average over 55 miles per day but we are not done counting yet, and remember about 100 of these miles are on foot with animals etc.

The scriptural evidence shows they arrived in Jerusalem at least 10 days before Pentecost. There are no indicators to indicate that they arrived at Jerusalem just-in-time for Pentecost which they could not do in 18 days no way. It says that when they reached Jerusalem the brethren received them gladly, Acts 21:17, and the NEXT DAY, verse 18, (This adds 1more day of no travel because it is still BEFORE Pentecost, a total of 33 no travel days) they went in unto James and the elders who informed them that there were many THOUSANDS of believing Jews that would here that he had come up to the feast and advised him to PURIFY himself with four men that had a vow on them in order to show that he was a Law keeper, and this he did the NEXT DAY, verse 26, a total of 34 no travel days during the traditional 50 day count and it is still not Pentecost.

NOTICE: some might try to say that this was Pentecost but the Scripture does not read that way and besides that why purify himself for 7 days AFTER Pentecost was over, to show them anything because the multitudes would be left for their journey home by then. Purifying is done BEFORE a feast as it says in John 11:55. The truth of the matter is that Paul arrived in plenty of time to purify himself with these men and the Scripture teaches that Pentecost had not occurred as of yet. Continuing on,

Then when 7 days was almost finished, some Jews from Asia, (Acts 21:27) who had come up for the feast, discover Paul in the temple and stirred up the MULTITUDE that had gathered in for Pentecost, so I will add another SIX DAYS to the 34 no travel days which bringing us to a total of 40 NO TRAVELING DAYS of the traditional 50 day count and it is still not Pentecost.

NOTICE: another indicator that Pentecost was not yet is because of the Jews from Asia, which was about 600 mi. away, were still there and so was the crowd or multitude that they stirred up who had also gathered for Pentecost. It is not likely all these people would have hung around Jerusalem for another 7 days after having arrived at least 7 days early for Pentecost.

If you read Acts -21:27 through 24:19 you will find another 2 days that Paul was in custody which brings the total to 42 DAYS OF NO TRAVELING before the traditional Pentecost, leaving only 8 TRAVEL DAYS to travel the 1000 miles from Philippi to Jerusalem.

Pentecost had not taken place until after Paul had been arrested and taken to Caesarea where the priest came down AFTER FIVE DAYS and the Jews from Asia didn't even show up; they probably had started their 600 mi. journey back home after Pentecost same as people do today, not hanging around another 7 or 8 days after Pentecost.

Paul was a Roman citizen, and they would not hold him any longer than necessary without allowing him to face his accusers. It is not a five-day journey from

Jerusalem to Caesarea and I believe that as soon as Pentecost and the new moon day was over the priest went down to accuse Paul. The Scripture just does not read or indicate that Pentecost was going on before Paul's arrest or before the 7 days of purification but even without these days the traditional Pentecost observed still have major problems.

You will see other indicators when you read it for yourself, with an unbiased mind of course.

And as I said before that even without the extra days at Jerusalem before Pentecost, it still won't do away with the fact that he could not have made it in time for the traditional Pentecost, even for those who count from the traditional Sabbath that they say falls within the days of unleavened bread.

Paul did not wait at Caesarea for many days and then leave so late as to arrive at Pentecost just in the neck of time. The following will show that many of the zealous Jews went up early for the 3 major feasts.

Paul was no less zealous than the Jews who had already gathered at Jerusalem and he did not leave in just enough time to barely get there for service, like some preachers today do. The Historian Josephus even tells how they went up 7 days early to purify themselves BEFORE the feast of Unleavened Bread.

In Josephus wars of the Jews pg. 742 Ch 5- (290) "when the people were come in great crowds to the feast of unleavened bread, on the EIGHTH DAY of the month Xanthicus [Nisan]," The foot note "e" in Josephus says that a week before Passover they went up to Jerusalem to PURIFY themselves, John 11:55 agrees with Josephus's quote.

We know that great crowds had gathered for Pentecost when James told Paul, "see how many thousands of Jews that believes" and we read a scriptural account of this in John 11:55,

"And the Jews' Passover was nigh at hand: and MANY went out of the country up to Jerusalem BEFORE the Passover, to PURIFY themselves"

This verse proves my point about the many zealous Jews that went up before these feasts. I believe the many that went up before the feast were the devout

Jews who were zealous of the LAW and we know that Pentecost commemorates the giving of the law or at least we can prove the law was given on the day that Aaron called a Chag/Pentecost, which was 50 days AFTER the 7th Sabbath. Ex-32:5

Here's another scripture in John which shows early arrivals for the major feasts.

John 12:1 is also in agreement with Josephus. "firsten our Saviour six days BEFORE the Passover came to Bethany, where Lazarus was which had been dead, whom he raised from the dead. 2There they made him a supper;"

Also remember how He went in and out of the temple and back and forth to Bethany each day before they took Him on the 14th?

These Historical quotes from Josephus and Scripture prove that many zealous Jews normally went up to Jerusalem before Pentecost and that's partly why James said that they were zealous toward the Law, (Pentecost) and that is why they went up early.

Paul was no less devout than these Jews and besides, it had been many years since he had last been up to Jerusalem and he said he must by all means keep this feast that cometh up at Jerusalem. This statement shows that Paul was not going up just to be on time for Pentecost, but to witness and fellowship with the brethren, before Pentecost and the fact that he abode MANY DAYS at Philips house in Caesarea shows that he was ahead of schedule and that he had plenty of time to arrive at Jerusalem a week or so before Pentecost to accomplish his intent.

Paul's desire was to keep Pentecost at Jerusalem if possible. The reason Paul said, if possible, is because the catching of ships and weather was uncertain, not to mention the possibility of unfavorable winds and other delays that might occur, and having to depend on someone-else he said if possible. But having reached Tyre and Caesarea, it is evident that Paul had a prosperous journey and was ahead of schedule after favorable winds etc. and having found ship's without having to wait too long. The Scripture shows that he was well ahead of schedule because he stayed 7 days at Tyre and many days at Caesarea and this he would not have done, had he not made good time.

The following is for those who after finding out that it is mathematically impossible for Paul to have kept the traditional Pentecost 50 days after the wave sheaf, and began hollering that Paul did not make it to Pentecost and instead of rethinking their position on Leviticus 23:16 to number 50 days after the 7th Sabbath, I submit the following which shows he did make it to Pentecost as he intended.

The way to prove this is we read that Paul was warned, by the Spirit at Tyre, Acts 21:4, not to go up to Jerusalem and again at Caesarea by Agabus the prophet, Acts 21:10 – 14. This not only shows that Paul and company were ahead of schedule on their journey to Jerusalem to keep Pentecost but that they had NOT BROKEN THE JOURNEY from Philippi to Jerusalem for Pentecost or they would not have kept warning Paul not to go up there in the above-mentioned Scriptures if he had broken his journey. This is important to show that they accomplished their desire to make it to Jerusalem for Pentecost but not the traditional Pentecost.

All anyone-has to do in order to see that Paul and company were still headed to Jerusalem to keep the SAME

Pentecost that they had set out to keep, after leaving Philippi, is to read the running account in Acts chapter 20 through chapter 21:4 and 21:4 says the disciples at Tyre, through the Spirit, told Paul that he should not go up to Jerusalem. At this point 1 would argue that the push for keeping Pentecost had not changed.

The next 7 versus shows that 2 or 3 days later, after receiving this warning, Paul reached Philips's house in Caesarea and AGAIN received another warning from Agabus the Prophet, further warning him not to go up to Jerusalem. These warnings against going up to Jerusalem is for the SAME trip and this shows that Paul left Caesarea to keep Pentecost in Jerusalem, as was his intention from Philippi. It's that simple when you read the Scripture with an unbiased mind.

Paul also made it known to Agabus the prophet and everyone that he was going to CONTINUE his journey and go up to Jerusalem for Pentecost and was willing to die also, if necessary.

There is nothing to suggest that Paul and company did not make it to Jerusalem in plenty of time for the true Pentecost and I know of no scholar that even suggests such a thing. And the evidence conclusively show that the traditional Pentecost is IMPOSSIBLE according to Scripture. Only someone-who does not understand that the true Pentecost is 50 days after the 7th Sabbath would even suggest that they did not make it to Pentecost, after reading Acts chapters 20 and 21.

In conclusion I may have made an error a day or 2 on 1side or the other which will not change the outcome. The evidence shows that Paul and Company along with many thousands of Jews and proselytes at Jerusalem observing Pentecost BEYOND the traditional 50-day count.

The traditional count is IMPOSSIBLE and as Sherlock Holmes says, "when the impossible has been removed, whatever remains, however improbably, must be the truth".

The apostle Paul and the others were actual eyewitnesses to a later Pentecost which is in harmony with Leviticus 23:16 and the rest of the Scriptures. I can also present over 1 million other eyewitnesses from the children of Israel in the wilderness. I will demonstrate in another chapter how that the children of Israel also COULD NOT have made it to Mount Sinai for the traditional Pentecost in 50 days according to Scripture and when they did make it, the law was given to Moses after numbering 50 days AFTER the 7th Sabbath and it was the exact same day that Aaron said was a feast/chag to YHWH, compare Exodus 32:5, Deuteronomy 9:11 and Exodus 31:18.

Chapter 3

Acts 1:5

Some have asked the question, doesn't Acts 1:5 favor the traditional count to Pentecost? "...ye shall be baptized with the Holy Ghost not many days hence."

At first glance it looks that way, but in reality, it actually disproves the traditional count to Pentecost!

We have already seen where Pentecost was being observed beyond the traditional 50-day count, making the traditional Pentecost impossible, and when the Holy Spirit was poured out in the Book of Acts, it was no different, because it too was also beyond the traditional 50-day count, because there were over 50 days passed before he even told his disciples to go tarry at Jerusalem to receive the Holy Spirit!!!

Again, the Holy Spirit was poured out on the day of Pentecost, while the disciples were waiting in the upper room, but before they were told to go there, more than 50 days had already passed, making the traditional 50 days from the wave sheaf count impossible!

The key is found in John 20:1 through 21:1-14, which shows there were 40 days that he was seen of the Apostles and he taught them, but the scriptures teaches that there were other days that he was not seen of the apostles, in addition to the 40 days that he was seen of them, before being received up into heaven, which is beyond the traditional 50-day count!

It says that from the first time they saw him, eight days past before he was seen the second time, and then it doesn't say how many days passed before Peter decided to go fishing, but we know it would have taken at least 4- or 5-days nonstop travel days. This is at least 13 days no seen of the apostles and when added to the 40 days seen of the apostles, is 53 days, which proves the traditional 50-day count is incorrect.

Below are some of my notes on the subject.

Acts 1:2–3 says, "Until the day in which the Messiah was taken up, after he had given Commandments unto the apostles whom he had chosen, and to whom he also showed himself alive after his passion "by many infallible proofs", "being seen of "them" 40 days, and speaking of the things pertaining to the kingdom of the Almighty:"

The many infallible proofs are the being seen alive, 40 times, by the apostles.

This raises a major question, were there any other days [in addition to the 40] that he was not seen of them, the apostles, before he was taken up???

The answer to the above question is yes, it is found by backing up to John 20:1 through 21:1-14, which gives the whole account, and teaches that OVER 50 days had passed, before he even told the disciples to go to Jerusalem and wait, again, making the traditional Pentecost count impossible, and showing Leviticus 23:16 is correct when it says to number the 50 days

True Count to Pentecost

AFTER the seventh Sabbath, not 50 days after the wave sheaf!

We see at least 13 days in which he was not seen of the apostles, in addition to the 40 days that he was seen of them, and this makes the traditional Pentecost impossible, because when you add 13 days that he was not seen of the apostles, to the 40 days that he was seen of them, you have over 50 days, not even counting the days in which he told them to go tarry at Jerusalem until they receive power from on high!

John 20:19 was the "first time" he appeared to the apostles, but Thomas was not with them, the "second time" was "after eight days" before he was seen of them again, John 20:26, and the "third time" was "at least "**five**" days after this", counting "at least **four** days" for the 80 mile journey from Jerusalem to the sea of Tiberius, and one day that they "fished all night" to the "next morning", before they seen him for the "3rd **time**", John 21:1 through verse 14.

This timeline is a very generous count, not even allowing another day or so for stopping for sleep, or food, and allowing 20 miles per day, nonstop.

Many days had passed before they seen him the "third time" at the sea of Tiberius, John 21:1-14.

John 21:1,14 KJV says,
[1] "After these things Jesus shewed himself again to the disciples at the sea of Tiberias; and on this wise shewed he himself...... [14] This is now the "**third time**" that Jesus shewed himself to his disciples, "**after**" that he was risen from the dead."

There's no telling how many days were in between the second and third sighting, but we have pinpointed enough days to kill the traditional Pentecost.

This all proves that the traditional Pentecost theory of numbering 1 day AFTER the seventh Sabbath instead of 50 days after the seventh Sabbath according to Leviticus 23:16, is impossible. Remember Pentecost means 50 not 1.

At any rate my following notes reveals that there were at least 13 days during which the apostles did not see him after his resurrection and when you add these 13 days to the 40 days that they did see him is a total of 53 days which is beyond the traditional Pentecost count and they still had to go to Jerusalem and tarry for the Holy Spirit that they were to receive not many days hence or after that, Acts 1:5, and it does not say how long they tarried, it could have been 40 days.

When we read Ac 13:30 "But God raised him from the dead:" and Ac 13:31 says, "And he was seen MANY DAYS of them which came up with him from Galilee to Jerusalem, who are his witnesses unto the people." We understand that he was seen MANY DAYS and when we read Acts 1:3 it tells us that MANY INFALLIBLE PROOFS CAN REFER TO 40 DAYS. One place that says he was beaten with MANY STRIPES in another place it says 40 stripes save one, indicating that many can be 40, and when it says, "not many days hence", could be saying, not 40 days from now.

Let's turn to Acts 1:3, and zero in on the verse and see if we can understand what it is actually saying. Acts 1:3 says, "to "whom" also He showed himself alive "after" his passion/sufferings by many infallible proofs, being "seen of them" 40 days, "and" speaking of things pertaining to the kingdom of God:"

Did he really show himself alive by many infallible proofs, being seen of them 40 days?

In other words, was He seen of them 40 days or was the showing himself alive by many infallible proofs referring to being seen of them several times DURING 40 days?

What were the infallible proofs of His being alive? Was it being seen 40 days or several sightings during a 40-day period?

I believe that showing himself alive 40 times was the infallible proofs.

It teaches he showed himself alive "after" his sufferings by "many" infallible proofs. How did He do that?

How did he show himself alive and what were the infallible proofs?

What is more of an infallible proof, being seen several times during 40 days, or 40 separate conclusive proofs or sightings of showing himself alive?

To whom did he show himself alive by these many infallible proofs?

I believe it was speaking of the apostles.

Is Acts 1:3 specifically speaking of the apostles whom He had chosen, when it says "being seen of THEM" 40 days?

Did the apostles see Him alive MANY or MORE in number of times than anyone else???

The Greek words for "many" means more in quantity or more in number and if being seen of THEM 40 days is SPECIFICALLY referring to the apostles whom he had chosen, it will add more days because we know from Scripture that the women saw him a day before the apostles saw him, assuming the first day of the week ends at evening when the apostles were gathered and the doors being shut in fear of the Jews when he appeared to the apostles for the first day of the 40 days.

Acts 1:3 specifically teaches He was seen 40 days of the apostles WHOM HE HAD CHOSEN and John 20:19 through 21:14 conclusively shows that He was

True Count to Pentecost

not seen of the apostles during at least 13 days and when we add the 40 days that he was seen of the apostles to the 13 days he was not seen of them it comes to a total of 53 days, not to mention the days that they were to tarry in Jerusalem until they were baptized with the Holy Spirit NOT MANY days hence, which had to be at least 2 more days, totaling 54 days.

This is conclusive proof that the true feast of Pentecost is beyond the traditional 50-day count, which harmonizes with the other proofs of them keeping Pentecost beyond the traditional count, that have already I presented.

It is easy to count the conclusive days that he was not seen of the apostles and add them to the days that he was seen of the apostles.

I will now show how you can prove the days or times he was not seen.

The first day in which he was seen of the apostles was the SECOND DAY after his resurrection at the close of the first day of the week at evening/17th which means he was not seen by the apostles during the first day after the resurrection. He was seen first of the women on the first day of the week, John 20:1 through 18 and then on the same first day of the week at evening, verse 19 which is actually the beginning of the second day of the week/17th to those of us who end the day at evening and this was the FIRST DAY of the 40 days that he showed himself alive to the apostles as Acts 1:3 clearly says. The apostle Thomas was not with them at this time, verse 24 but AFTER EIGHT DAYS later he showed himself alive the SECOND TIME to the apostles whom he had chosen and Thomas was with them, verse 26. He was not seen of them DURING THE SEVEN DAYS before the eighth day that he appeared to them the second time. This is a TOTAL OF EIGHT DAYS so far and only TWO times or infallible proofs of showing himself alive. The THIRD DAY of the 40 days or time he showed himself alive or was seen of the apostles was at the sea of Galilee/Tiberias which is a FOUR DAYS journey from Jerusalem according to several web searches on distance's and it does not say how many days later it was but even if they immediately went straight to the sea without going home etc, and went fishing immediately after traveling the four nonstop day journey it was still the next morning that he appeared or showed himself alive to the apostles for the THIRD TIME or third day of the 40 days that he was seen of them, verse 4.

The map in the back of my Bible shows the trip to be over 70 miles, some say over 100, but all agreed that it was at least four days journey.

At any rate this is a total of at least 13 DAYS that he was NOT seen of the apostles in addition to the 40 days that he was seen or showed himself alive to the apostles, not counting the seventh day's journey from Mount Olivet and the days they were to wait for the promise of the Holy Spirit at Jerusalem.

It was actually the NEXT MORNING that the third appearance took place after they fished through the night according to verse 4, therefore we have a total of at least 13 conclusive days in which he was not seen of the apostles after his resurrection and when you add this to the 40 days that he showed himself alive to them is a total of 53 days.

And reading on, John 21:14 actually says "this is now the THIRD TIME that the Messiah showed himself (ALIVE) to his disciples, after that he was risen from the dead" or "showed himself alive". i.e., these 3 appearances where he showed himself alive is 3 of the many/40 infallible proofs or showing himself alive spoken of in Acts 1:3 where it says,

Ac 1:3 "To whom also he shewed himself alive after his passion by many infallible proofs, "being" seen of them forty days, and speaking of the things pertaining to the kingdom of YHWH:"

The "whom" and "them" is SPECIFICALLY referring to the apostles and the 40 days of appearances to them are the many infallible proofs or Certainty's.

Notice he not only showed himself alive after the resurrection but spoke to them things pertaining to the kingdom.

At any rate when you add 12 and 40 together it is a total of 53 days which is beyond the traditional Pentecost, and they still have to go to Jerusalem and wait for the promise which was to be not many days hence. This has to be at least two more days making a total of 54 days, which makes the traditional 50 days from the wave sheaf Pentecost impossible.

This also shows that we are to number the 50 days AFTER the seventh Sabbath instead of 50 days after the wave sheaf according to Leviticus 23:16. This is the only way to harmonize these Scriptures along with MANY others.

The Book of Acts can cause us to think that they returned and went into the upper room and stayed there for several days until the Holy Spirit was poured out, but the gospel of Luke says they returned to Jerusalem and were continually in the temple praising and blessing the Almighty, Luke 24:53.

In other words, they may have gone straight to the upper room but not to receive the Holy Spirit at that time according to Luke's Gospel. And when they did receive the Holy Spirit in the upper room they were scattered abroad and not continually in the temple at Jerusalem. Therefore, they could have been weeks of tarrying at Jerusalem before they went into the upper room to receive the Holy Spirit.

There could have been weeks before he appeared to them the third time at the Sea of Galilee etc., we do not know but we do know from the above Scriptures that it was above the traditional 50-day count before the Holy Spirit was poured out on the day of Pentecost.

Again, to those of us who end the day at evening, we know that after the resurrection he was first seen of the women and was not seen by the apostles until AFTER the first day at evening. i.e., the 16th day at evening which is the beginning of the 17th day of the first month same as the 7 days of unleavened bread begins on the 14th day at evening which is the beginning of the 15th, and the Day of Atonement is on 10th day but begins on the 9th day at evening which is the beginning of the 10th.

Therefore, the same first day at evening/16th is the second day/17th. Therefore the 40 days were referring to days in which He SPECIFICALLY showed himself alive to the apostles after the resurrection as Acts 1:3 states, "being seen of them [the apostles] 40 days".

Either He was seen of the apostles 40 days, or he was not. We know from the above that he was not seen of them 40 days in a row and there were days that he was not seen of them at all.

Side note: The traditional count always consists of 50 days therefore you would not have to count to Pentecost because it would always be on the same day.

The scriptural Pentecost is 101- or 102-days dependent on whether there is one day between the Sabbath and new moon and therefore you have to count for it because it does not always fall out on the day next to the Sabbath as indicated by Josephus.

If this did not happen it would be on a fixed date same as the other two feast and there would be no need to count to Pentecost, you would know what date it is every year, especially for those who correctly begin the count from the 16th. And those who begin the count from the Morrow after the traditional Sabbath that falls within the days of unleavened bread will always know it to be on a Sunday and they will not have to count either.

The true Pentecost keepers will have to count even if they calculate ahead.

The 40 days that He was seen or showed himself alive to the apostles were infallible proofs of his resurrection. i.e., being seen so many times.

He was seen of them on 40 different occasions from the time of his resurrection to his ascension into the heavens. If Acts 1:3 is not referring to the number of times he was seen by the apostles as proofs of his resurrection and only referring to a number of days from the time of his resurrection would not be proofs. i.e., just saying he was alive for a distance of 40 days before he ascended up and not being seen of the apostles 40 different days is not as much proof.

His appearing to the apostles on 40 different days or occasions was the infallible proofs by showing himself alive.

This is not speaking of a distance of 40 days to show proof of his being alive but the number of times he appeared to the apostles and spoke to them things pertaining to the kingdom.

Joh 20:16 the Messiah saith unto her, Mary. She turned herself, and saith unto him, Rabboni; which is to say, Master.

Joh 20:17 the Messiah saith unto her, Touch me not; for I am not yet ascended to my Father: but go to my brethren, and say unto them, I ascend unto my Father, and your Father; and to my G-d, and your G-d.

Joh 20:18 Mary Magdalene came and told the disciples that she had seen the Master, and that he had spoken these things unto her.

Joh 20:19 Then the same day at evening, being the first day of the week, when the doors were shut where the disciples were assembled for fear of the Jews, came the Messiah, and stood in the midst, and saith unto them, Peace be unto you.

Joh 20:24 But Thomas, one of the twelve, called Didymus, was not with them when the Messiah came.

Joh 20:26 And "after eight days" "again" his disciples were within, and Thomas with them: then came the

Messiah, the doors being shut, and stood in the midst, and said, Peace be unto you.

Joh 21:1 After these things the Messiah shewed himself "again" to the disciples at the sea of Tiberias; and on this wise shewed he himself....

Joh 21:14 "This is now the "third time" that the Messiah shewed himself (ALIVE) to his disciples, after that he was risen from the dead."

Ac 1:1 "The former treatise have I made, O Theophilus, of all that the Messiah began both to do and teach,

Ac 1:2 Until the day in which he was taken up, after that he through the Holy Ghost had given commandments unto the apostles whom he had chosen:

Ac 1:3 To whom also he "shewed himself alive" after his passion by many infallible proofs, being seen of them forty days, and speaking of the things pertaining to the kingdom of God:

Ac 1:4 And, being assembled together with them, commanded them that they should not depart from

Jerusalem, but wait for the promise of the Father, which, saith he, ye have heard of me.

Ac 1:5 For John truly baptized with water; but ye shall be baptized with the Holy Ghost not many days hence."

Definition of INFALLIBLE PROOFS
Strong's Greek Dictionary
5039. tekmerion
τεκμηριον tekmerion tek-may'-ree-on
neuter of a presumed derivative of tekmar (a goal or fixed limit); a token (as defining a fact), i.e., criterion [or/decisive factor/reason/standard] of certainty:--infallible proof.

The TOKEN or Defining a fact was Him being seen a NUMBER of days or times by the apostles whom He had chosen, not a space of time. Infallible proofs must meet certain criteria i.e., a criterion i.e. care of certainty which equals a decisive factor of him being seen ALIVE after the crucifixion/passion 40 days or times by the apostles.

The apostles seen him more in number of times or days than anyone else.

Side note: I believe the word "and" is a conjunctive word tying the speaking of the things pertaining to the kingdom to the being seen of them 40 days. i.e., speaking the things pertaining to the kingdom during the 40 days of his appearing to them.

I believe 40 days is significant same as the 40 days the Almighty taught Moses in the Mount just before the law was given to Moses on the day of Pentecost which was at the end of 40 days and 40 nights, [not the beginning of it] Deuteronomy 9:11 and Exodus 31:18, the Messiah specifically taught his disciples for the same number of days before Pentecost.

Perhaps I will finish this later, but for now I have said enough.

Chapter 4

The Hebrew Word for unto/until in Leviticus 23:16 is "ad"

Some try to argue the Hebrew word "ad", unto/until supports counting 50 days from the wave sheaf instead of 50 days AFTER the seventh Sabbath, Leviticus 23:16, but this is not true.

Even Hebrew scholars such as Rashi agree that the Hebrew word "AD" means up unto or until a certain point but "**not including that point**". If you count seven Sabbaths up unto or until the morrow after the seventh Sabbath, that is only 49 days, because the Morrow, or next day, is not included in the count of the Seven Sabbaths, and 7 times 7 is 49, not 50.

You go up until the beginning of the Morrow, or next day, which is only 49 days, not 50, as some would like for it to be, and then you number 50 days instead of numbering "one day".

Again, even the famous Hebrew scholar Rashi along with many others agree that the Morrow after the seventh Sabbath is not included in the count because of the Hebrew word for "unto" or "until", see Rashi's commentary on Leviticus 23:16.

Now if you count seven Sabbaths complete up unto or until the morrow after the seventh Sabbath and INCLUD the morrow after the seventh Sabbath, that would be 50 days, BUT it would make the counting of the seven Sabbaths INEXACT because seven traditional Sabbaths is 49 days not 50 days!

According to Scripture the morrow after the seventh Sabbaths is not included in the count of the seven Sabbaths, i.e., it would NOT be seven Sabbaths complete if you included the next day after the seventh Sabbath!

And on top of that you would have to change the meaning of the Hebrew word for UNTIL because it means up until a point but not counting that point.

Again, it is the seven Sabbaths that are complete up until the Morrow after the seventh Sabbath NOT the 50 days!

We must count seven Sabbaths first, and then "number" either 1 day or 50 days before bringing the new grain offering, and the Scripture teaches to number 50 days after the seventh Sabbath NOT 1 day, and then bring it (Lev-23:16), and that's the way the children of Israel and Nature, understood it, as we will see shortly, remember Pentecost means 50 not 1, and remember also that the children of Israel were eyewitnesses and were there living it.

In discussing this subject, it will also help to understand that Pentecost is the first fruits of the wheat harvest, and there are TWO wheat harvests in the world today. You might ask what has two wheat harvests have to do with anything.

The answer to this is that Pentecost is the firstfruits of wheat harvest and there is one wheat harvest in the spring, about two weeks after Barley harvest, and one in the "summer" about 50 more days after the one in the spring or after the seventh Sabbath is counted, which is the true Pentecost wheat harvest.

You cannot find in Scripture a wheat harvest two weeks after the barley harvest. This brings us to the question,

Chapter 5

Which Of the Two Wheat Harvests (That Are in the World Today) Is The Scriptural Pentecost Wheat Harvest of old???

First of all, as we have demonstrated, Scripture does not support a third month wheat harvest. As a matter of fact, **there is not a harvest "of any kind" in the third month** in Scripture. I challenge anyone to find even one. This is an embarrassment to a third month Pentecost.

Most people, not being farmers, do not realize that they are TWO types of wheat harvests in the world today, and we know from Scripture that Pentecost is the firstfruits of a wheat harvest. It is the duty of the serious truth seekers to find out which of these TWO wheat harvests was originally used for the Pentecost firstfruits.

As I said, one of these wheat harvests takes place in the spring around the second and third month and the other wheat harvest takes place in the summer around the end of the fourth month or the beginning of the fifth, which is comparable to our mid-July to mid-August.

Again, the only conclusive wheat harvest found in Scripture is the **summer** wheat harvest that takes place after the seventh Sabbath is counted and the 50 days are numbered, and not 50 days after the wave sheaf. See more in the chapter on summer wheat harvest.

Leviticus 23:16 has been a major topic for those opposing the fourth month Pentecost which is from the summer wheat harvest in favor of the traditional Pentecost in the third month from the winter wheat harvest. The wheat they are using for the traditional Pentecost, which is not found in Scripture, takes "six or seven months" to harvest and our Savior teaches in John 4:35 that it is "four months" to harvest.

True Count to Pentecost

The Winter Wheat is sown in the fall, around September or October, and reaped six or seven months later in the springtime, about two weeks after Barley harvest.

The Summer Wheat is sown in the "true springtime" and reaped in the summer, four months later. This is the true Pentecost wheat and our Savior himself indicates that there are FOUR MONTHS then cometh the harvest, John 4:35 but with the winter wheat in takes SIX or SEVEN MONTHS till harvest.

Notice I said "true Springtime", which is a month before the traditional spring time, and this is another subject altogether, but true spring time begins around February 19, and not March 20, go to my website at http://lunarsabbath.info/id43.html and see True Equinox

Again, they focus on the Hebrew word UNTIL and think that is support their position while ignoring the fact that the only conclusive wheat harvest found in Scripture is in the **summer**, NOT spring. Again, see chapter on summer wheat harvest.

They also ignore the fact that in Scripture there is not even a harvest OF ANY KIND in the third month, neither is there a feast/chag mentioned in the third month, from Genesis to Revelations, don't you think these facts should be worth something in our search for truth???

Or should we not even consider them and hold the traditions of men instead?

There is a conclusive feast/chag declared in the end of the fourth month, and it was exactly after counting 50 days after the 7th Sabbath which we will see shortly. Amazing!

Keep in mind that the word Chag, is a special Hebrew word and only refers to the 3 major feasts, unleavened bread, Pentecost, and the feast of Tabernacles, it is not used any other way in scripture.

Leviticus 23:15-16 says, "you shall COUNT unto you from the morrow after the Sabbath from the day that you brought the sheaf of the wave offering; seven Sabbaths shall be complete: Even unto/until the morrow AFTER the seventh Sabbath SHALL YOU

NUMBER 50 days; AND YE SHALL OFFER a new meat offering unto YHWH".

If we were to number 50 days AFTER the seventh Sabbath complete, it would obviously bring us to a new meat offering of the **summer** wheat harvest, which is 50 days beyond the **spring** wheat harvest. But if we numbered ONE day after the seventh Sabbath complete it would obviously bring us to a spring wheat harvest of the winter wheat, which is not even found in Scripture. This is an absolute.

There are three major feasts each year and with the traditional counting of one day after the seven Sabbaths will cause TWO of the three major feasts to fall in the springtime, NONE in the summertime, and one in the fall season but the Scripture teaches they are to be observed in their SEASONS, each feast has "its own" season. Here's what the traditional count looks like,

1 - 3 - - - 7, see how uneven or spaced out the trips to Jerusalem would be?

Now here's what YHWH'S count looks like,

1 - - 4 - - 7, see how they are equally spaced out through the year and in "their own" seasons, as Scripture teaches, with no bumps and skips, compared to man's tradition which has two of the feasts in one season instead of each Feast in its own season.

His feasts are held three **times**/seasons in the year, **spring**, **summer,** and **fall**. Not **"spring", "spring",** and **fall** which is only two times or seasons that the 3 feasts are held in.

If we do it his way the feast will be spread out more evenly and the people will have an extra 50 days after Passover before they turn around and go back up to Jerusalem. They will have 100 days after Passover instead of 50 days before they have to make a trip back up to Jerusalem again. YHWH spaces out the feasts more evenly than man does, which is much easier on the people.

Chapter 6

Punctuation marks

The **REAL** question is, how did ancient Israel number???

Did they number 1 day, or 50 days AFTER the seventh Sabbath complete, i.e., which of the TWO wheat harvest is the scripture referring to???

Remember also that punctuation marks were not in the original Hebrew text but were later added by translators etc., depending on how they felt the verse should read. You can move or add one punctuation mark in Lev-23:15 and 16 and it will read very different. Try it for yourself. Here are a few examples of how it would read by punctuating it differently.

"you shall COUNT unto you from the morrow after the Sabbath, from the day that you brought the sheaf of the wave offering, seven Sabbaths shall be complete even unto/until the morrow AFTER the seventh Sabbath. YOU SHALL NUMBER 50 days AND YE SHALL OFFER a new meat offering unto YHWH."

This clearly shows that you number the 50 days AFTER the 7th Sabbath instead of the wave sheaf.

Or you could move one semicolon and it would read, Leviticus 23:15-16 "you shall COUNT unto you from the morrow after the Sabbath from the day that you brought the sheaf of the wave offering; seven Sabbaths shall be complete even unto/until the morrow AFTER the seventh Sabbath; YOU SHALL NUMBER 50 days AND YE SHALL OFFER a new meat offering unto YHWH.

I think the first example is the correct way and the "shall ye" and "ye shall" is saying the same thing in Hebrew. At any rate, the punctuation marks were added and were not in the original.

Again, it is the seven Sabbaths that are complete up **until** the Morrow after the seventh Sabbath NOT the 50 days that are complete! Seven Sabbaths is not 50 days.

I will quote from the Septuagint on Leviticus 23:15-16, which says,

15, "and ye shall number to yourselves from the day after the Sabbath, from the day on which you shall offer the sheaf of the heave offering, "seven full weeks": until the morrow "after the last week" ye shall number 50 days", and "ye shall" bring the new meat offering to YHWH." i.e. After counting those seven weeks, ye shall number the 50 days and then bring the meat offering which would be from the summer wheat harvest. You do not number 1 day after counting the seven Sabbaths but instead you number 50 days after the Seventh Sabbath.

We can do the same with the Greek Septuagint as we did with the Hebrew and add a period after week and it will read,

"and ye shall number to yourselves from the day after the Sabbath, from the day on which you shall offer the sheaf of the heave offering, "seven full weeks" until the morrow "after the last week. "Ye shall number 50 days", and "ye shall" bring the new meat offering to YHWH." i.e., after those seven weeks you shall number 50 days, NOT 1 day. Ferrar Fenton in The Ferrar Fenton Bible actually reads this way, it Says,

"You shall also count for yourselves from the day after the Sabbath that you bring the wave sheaf, seven Sabbaths. They must be complete. **Then after the seventh Sabbath, you shall count fifty days**, when you shall present a new offering to the EVERY LIVING" Leviticus 23:15-16.

We must also remember the word "shall ye" or "ye shall" is ALWAYS "future tense" and never past tense therefore the numbering of the 50 days comes AFTER the seventh Sabbath are counted.

It does not say that the morrow after the seventh Sabbath you **"have"** numbered 50 days, but you **"shall"** number 50 days, there's a big difference, you shall number (future) the 50 days, after the seventh sabbath complete.

If we sit Leviticus 23:16 to the side for a minute and go on to the scriptures and see how the Ancient Israelites interpreted this verse, it should end the Pentecost debate forever because surely, they understood the Hebrew words.

Unfortunately, most people are not willing to do this because they are more loyal to their tradition, preacher, organization, denomination, etc. than they are the Word of YHWH, and will follow the blind leaders, no matter what the Scripture teaches and how the Ancient Israelites understood the verse and that is so sad, but true.

Scripture will interpret Scripture and the evidence is conclusive that the children of Israel understood that they were to count 50 days **AFTER** the seventh Sabbath, NOT 1 day. They were NOT to count 50 days from the wave sheaf but instead they were to count 50 days from the Morrow after the seventh Sabbath, and the first fruit of the wheat would be from the **summer** wheat harvest, not a spring wheat harvest which cannot even be found in Scripture.

Let's examine Scripture and get the **testimonies from thousands of eyewitnesses** who were actually there, and who actually carried out the command of

Leviticus 23:16 as to what they were to do when they came into the land.

Remember also that the first fruits of the new meat offering was to be from THEIR LABORS that THEY SOWED in the field (Ex-23: 16), and when they came into the land and reaped the harvest there of, they would naturally sow the land for future crops, which if they sowed in the first month when they come into the land, they could reap the firstfruits after counting seven sabbaths and THEN numbering 50 days, but they could not reap a first fruit in 50 days, because it is AGRICULTURALLY IMPOSSIBLE to reap the firstfruits of a wheat harvest in 50 days, after sowing, summer wheat takes about 120 days to harvest, not 50, and this alone disproves the traditional third month Pentecost.

Know this also, Aaron, YHWH'S High Priest, and the children of Israel were eyewitnesses as to how Leviticus 23:16 should be interpreted and carried out and they obviously counted 50 days AFTER the seventh Sabbath complete, BECAUSE when Aaron declared the feast/Chag to YHWH, it was in the end of the fourth month at the time of the summer wheat harvest, NOT the beginning of the third month at the winter wheat harvest that takes place in the spring.

This is found in Exodus 32:5 where Aaron said tomorrow is a chag/feast to YHWH. The Hebrew word "feast/chag", is only used for one of the three major feasts each year as we will show later and the Law was actually given at the end of Moses' 40 days and 40 nights in the mount, which was 50 days AFTER the seventh Sabbath, and not in the third month, 50 days after the wave sheaf as the traditional Pentecost keepers suggest. And as I said, it was the exact same day that the Law that YHWH had written with his own finger, was given to Moses, (**Ex-31:18** and **Deut- 9:11).** which we will also show later.

Chapter 7

Aaron and Pentecost

Some try to argue that Aaron did not know that tomorrow was Pentecost. Not only did Aaron know about Pentecost but all the elders and the children of Israel knew about it also because in Exodus 20:22 and 21:1 YHWH instructed Moses what to tell the children of Israel and reading through to Exodus 23:14 – 16 it says …. "Three times thou shall keep a feast to me in the year". YHWH names the feasts, Feast of Unleavened Bread, Feast of Firstfruits/Pentecost, and Feast of Ingatherings/Tabernacles, and then instructs Moses to relate them to the people. Therefore, Aaron and the people knew when Pentecost was while Moses was in the mount. Also in Exodus 24:3 it says that Moses came and told the people all the words of YHWH, and all the judgments and this was BEFORE he went into the mountain for 40 days and 40 nights as verse four through nine of the same chapter proves. So, when Aaron says "tomorrow is a feast/chag to YHWH" he knew about it. Perhaps the people were impatient when they murmured saying "where is Moses" because same as Aaron they also knew the next day was Pentecost and supposed he should be back by then getting ready for it and they were worrying.

We could stop this little book here and it should be more than enough to convince the honest truth seeker that Leviticus 23:16 should be understood to count 50 days AFTER the seventh Sabbath and that the traditional Pentecost is bogus and is nothing more than the tradition of men, but we will continue with much more conclusive evidence and even examples where people in both the old and New Testament actually observed Pentecost **beyond** the traditional 50 day count.

Chapter 8

Law Given on Pentecost

Most people agree that Pentecost commemorates the giving of the law and as I said earlier, the law was not given, signed sealed and delivered until the END of the 40 days and 40 nights which is 50 days after the seventh Sabbath, not 50 days at the wave sheaf. See Exodus 31:18 and Deuteronomy 9:11, where Moses testifies that the law was given to him at the END of the 40 days and 40 nights, not at the beginning.

Moses was not even on the mount when the law was spoken in the third month but was in the camp with the people, which I will deal with later. Every one of YHWH's feasts commemorates something including Pentecost. The feast of Unleavened Bread in the first and Tabernacles in the seventh month commemorates being delivered from Egypt's bondage when they ate

Unleavened Bread and dwelt in booths/Tabernacles and the only thing around the time of Pentecost was when the children of Israel were given the law at Mt. Sinai and each of these feasts are commemorated around the time of a major harvests and therefore Pentecost has to commemorate the giving of the law around the time of the **summer wheat harvest**. I believe the new moon day commemorates the creation of Heaven and Earth when everything was dark BEFORE he said let there be light and worked on his creation for six days and the 7th day Sabbath commemorates His rest after working on his creation for six days. I believe the Day of Atonement commemorates the atonement that YHWH himself made for Adam and Eve's sins on the ninth day of creation at evening after the serpent tempted them on the ninth day in the garden. At any rate these feast days commemorates something and being as the Law was actually given after counting 50 days from the Morrow AFTER the seventh Lunar Sabbath complete why not let Pentecost commemorate it, especially since he allowed this to happen at the summer wheat harvest? go to our website at www.lunarsabbath.info where we show 72 pinpointed weekly Sabbaths in Scripture and offer a $10,000 reward for only one conclusive weekly Sabbath that cannot be intelligently argued against that was not on the 8th, 15th, 22nd, or 29th day of the moon/month.

See also how that the traditional uninterrupted unbroken cycle is MATHEMATICALLY IMPOSSIBLE because When Adam and Eve's Descendants migrated east and west from the Garden of Eden and meet 1000 or so years later on the opposite side of the Earth, they will be a full 24 hours apart in their Sabbath keeping if they were using the traditional uninterrupted cycle and they will have TWO uninterrupted unbroken Seventh day cycles each and every week when the Scripture teaches only one. You will have one cycle for the tribes that migrated east and one for the tribes that migrated west, and it will be a full day apart even though the two tribes are next door to each other or even in the same house. Even though it is the same cycle the tribes that traveled East will keep it before the Tribes that traveled West. This is an absolute that cannot be intelligently argued against, and this is why they created an imaginary man-made International Date Line to supposedly put them back on the same cycle which in reality it does not do. The only way the traditional unbroken cycle will work is if you have an imaginary man-made date line to break the cycle! Otherwise, people will be worshiping on "TWO" different Sabbath day cycles. Meditate on it a while and you will see. See full details and more on this at the above website. Now back to Pentecost.

Chapter 9

The Prophet Joel's Pentecost

The Prophet Joel when referring to the outpouring of the Holy Spirit on the day of Pentecost/firstfruits, says that the floors would be full of wheat and the wine presses full of wine, and this was fulfilled in the book of Acts where they were being accused of being drunk on the new wine. This had to be at the summer wheat harvest Pentecost because there is no new wine in the third month because it is AGRICULTURALLY IMPOSSIBLE to have any grapes in the wine presses or for the grapes to be ripe in the beginning of the third month for the traditional Pentecost as I said earlier. **See chapter on Joel and summer wheat harvest.**

Now back to the Hebrew word "until". My Bullinger lexicon gives the definition of the word until and says that the word "until" means, "as long as, marking the continuance of an action up to the time of another action".

We have an action of COUNTING seven Sabbath even unto the morrow after the seventh Sabbath and then we have another action of NUMBERING 50 days and then we have an action of bringing the new meat offering. The first action is to count the seven Sabbath and the next action is to number 50 days, not number one day, but 50 days. Pentecost means 50 not 1.

The first thing was to COUNT seven Sabbaths and the second thing they were to do was to NUMBER 50 days. The third thing they were to do was to offer a new meat offering to YHWH.

They were NOT instructed to COUNT seven Sabbaths complete **AND THEN** bring a new meat offering, as the traditional Pentecost observers do. They were instructed to count seven Sabbaths complete up "unto/until" the day after the seventh Sabbath, AND THEN number 50 days. Truly they were instructed to NUMBER 50 days but **NOT UNTIL** AFTER they counted seven Sabbaths first. They were instructed to offer a new meat offering but not until AFTER they numbered 50 days first which numbering began **AFTER** the seventh Sabbath complete. Some things are hidden in simplicity and in a moment, I will give you scriptural examples where the children of Israel understood it this way and actually observed a chag/feast 50 days AFTER the seventh Sabbath.

If the 50-day count were to begin from the wave sheaf, it would read, "even unto the morrow "after" the seventh Sabbath "shall ye bring a new meat offering", instead of numbering 50 days after the seventh Sabbath and then bring the new meat/grain offering! But He does not say shall ye offer a new meat offering "after" the seventh Sabbath, it says, **AFTER the seventh Sabbath shall ye number 50 days**, and THEN offer the new meat offering. This is a BIG BIG difference.

Chapter 10

NUMBERING

THEY ARE TWO COUNTS TO PENTECOST IN LEVITICUS 23:16

This chapter will conclusively prove from Scripture and Scripture along that there are TWO counts to Pentecost; one count is of seven Sabbaths and another count of 50 days, TWO separate counts. There is a difference between counting Sabbaths and numbering days. You can count seven trucks and then number 50 cars and then cross the street, but you do not cross the street until you count the seven trucks and then number the 50 cars. There is a difference between trucks and cars, same as there is a difference between Sabbaths and days and one is counted and the other numbered.

Before we look to see what the instructions in Leviticus 23 is saying, let's see what it is **NOT** saying.

It does NOT say that we are to count seven Sabbaths complete "AND THEN" offer a new meat offering, as the traditional Pentecost keepers try to make it say. You have to count seven Sabbaths complete "FIRST" and "then" NUMBER either **one day or 50 days** after the seventh Sabbath and the Scripture teaches to number 50 days, not one day and remember Pentecost means to number 50 days, not number one day!

Once again it does NOT say "even unto the morrow "after" the seventh Sabbath "shall ye" offer a new meat offering," but He did say "even unto the morrow "after" the seventh Sabbath "**shall ye number 50**" days and THEN offer a new meat offering, Leviticus 23:16, i.e., after the seventh Sabbath shall ye number 50 days, but not before. And THEN bring the new meat offering but not until you number the 50 days after the seventh Sabbath, and this is exactly what the children of Israel done. I know I sound redundant, but I want you to see how the children of Israel understood this verse and their actions in Exodus 32:5 proves it, along with the many other profound proofs which I will get to in a little while.

The morrow after the seventh Sabbath is **NOT** even a part of the first count because it says to count seven Sabbaths complete, even **"unto/until"** the morrow after the seventh Sabbath. i.e., the seventh Sabbath is complete at the BEGINNING of the morrow after the seventh Sabbath. As I said before, if you count seven Sabbaths up unto or until the morrow after the seventh Sabbath complete, the morrow is not included in the count and that is only 49 days, not 50, as some would like for it to be.

The traditions of men will try to blind your mind to the definition of these Hebrew words and also cause you to ignore the examples where thousands of Israelites observed Pentecost 50 days beyond the traditional Pentecost count which was at the time that the law and tables of stone was actually given to Israel.

Again, there are three things mentioned in the instructions concerning Pentecost,

Number one, ye shall COUNT seven Sabbaths complete,

Number two, ye shall NUMBER 50 days,

Number three and ye shall offer a new meat/grain offering to YHWH.

As I have said, you do **NOT** count seven Sabbaths complete and THEN bring a new meat offering, this is not Scripture, but instead you count seven Sabbaths complete up **unto** the end of the seventh Sabbath AND THEN number 50 days and "**THEN**" offer a new meat/grain offering, this is Scripture. The end of seven Sabbaths brings you to the starting point of the **SECOND** count which consists of 50 days and begins on the morrow after the seventh Sabbath complete. The first count consisted of seven Sabbaths and then ended. The second count consists of 50 days and then it ends and that is when you bring the new meat offering according to Leviticus 23:16 and it will be the same day that Aaron said was a chag in Exodus 32:6 and it will be the same day the law was given to Moses, and that is no coincidence.

Remember the first thing they were to do is count seven Sabbaths complete.

The second thing they were to do was to number 50 days.

The third thing they were to do was to offer a new meat offering.

Again! They were not instructed to count seven Sabbaths complete **AND THEN** offer a new meat offering, NO NO NO, but this is what the traditional Pentecost keepers do. They Count seven Sabbaths and then number ONE day, instead of 50 days and bring the new meat offering, instead of numbering 50 days after the seventh Sabbath complete, and then bring the new meat offering as the Scripture teaches.

They were instructed to count seven Sabbaths complete up "**UNTIL**" the day after the seventh Sabbath, and then they were instructed to number 50 days but **not until** after they counted seven Sabbaths first. They were instructed to offer a new meat offering but not until after they numbered 50 days which numbering began **AFTER** the seventh Sabbath complete. I know I am being redundant again, but tradition is hard to erase from our minds.

Again, if the 50-day count were to begin from the wave sheaf, it would read, "even unto the morrow "after" the seventh Sabbath "shall ye" bring a new meat offering". But He does not say that. He does not say "shall ye bring a new meat offering "after" the seventh Sabbath", it say's **after the seventh Sabbath shall ye number 50 days**, and **THEN** bring the new meat offering. You must get this in your mind because that was what was in the mind of the children of Israel according to Exodus 32:5 and other Scriptures such as Joel chapter 2 etc.

Every count must have a beginning and ending point, and I think we all agree that the beginning point for the seven Sabbaths complete begins on the morrow after the Sabbath/15th when the priest waves the wave sheaf/16th. The question is, where does this count, or action end and the next count or action begin?

As I have shown above, there are TWO counts mentioned in Leviticus 23 and they were not to offer the new meat offering until **"BOTH"** counts were completed.

If we count seven Sabbaths complete and "then" bring a new meat offering, we are partial in the Law, but if we count seven Sabbaths complete up unto the morrow after the seventh Sabbath and then number

50 days instead of one day and then bring the new meat offering, we have fulfilled the Law.

The Scripture says,

"Speak unto the children of Israel, and say unto them, When ye be come into the land which I give unto you, and shall reap the harvest thereof, then ye shall bring a sheaf of the firstfruits of your harvest unto the priest: [11]And he shall wave the sheaf before YHWH, to be accepted for you: on the morrow after the Sabbath/15th the priest shall wave it/16th. ...... [15]And ye shall count unto you from the morrow "**AFTER**" the Sabbath, from the day that ye brought the sheaf of the wave offering; seven Sabbaths shall be complete:[16]Even unto the morrow "**AFTER**" the seventh Sabbath SHALL YE NUMBER fifty days; and ye shall offer a new meat offering unto YHWH.

From the Morrow after the Sabbath, you are to number seven more Sabbaths all the way up unto the beginning of the next day after the seventh Sabbath.

The FIRST count goes up "**even**" unto/until the morrow after the seventh Sabbath and "**ENDS**", the SECOND count begins and goes through 50 days and the text is understood as saying, "the morrow after the seventh Sabbath shall ye number 50 days," one reason it is to be understood this way is because the morrow after the seventh Sabbath is "**NOT**" included in the first count of the seven Sabbaths, seven Sabbaths is not 50 days, the seven Sabbaths goes up until the beginning of the morrow after the seventh Sabbath and no further and "THEN" ye number 50 days and THEN you bring the new meat offering and not before. i.e., the first count goes even up to the morrow after the seventh Sabbaths complete then stops and then you NUMBER 50 days and bring a new meet offering. The seventh Sabbath complete end at the BEGINNING of the morrow or it is not a complete Sabbath.

Again, it is important to remember that the morrow after the seventh Sabbath is not included in the first count of the Sabbaths or the seven Sabbaths would be inexact as the Hebrew scholar Rashi says in his commentary on this verse.

So, the question is, when do we bring the new meat offering? Is it after we number 50 days? The answer is yes! But when do we begin to number the 50 days?

Do we number the 50 days from the morrow after the wave sheaf /16th? Or do we number the 50 days from the morrow AFTER the "seventh" Sabbath complete? Read Leviticus 23:16 in this light and you will have your answer. You are NOT to NUMBER "one" day after the seventh Sabbath complete but you number 50 days after the seventh Sabbath complete.

The Scripture says, "Even unto the morrow AFTER the seventh Sabbath shall you number 50 days; and ye shall offer a new meat offering unto YHWH." Leviticus 23:16. How much plainer can it get? Because of their tradition most people forget the Hebrew and English grammar when it comes to this verse.

The children of Israel obviously understood it like it says, i.e., number 50 days AFTER the seventh Sabbath because they celebrated it exactly 50 days after the seventh lunar Sabbath according to Exodus 32:5.

They celebrated the feast at the proper time, but they were to celebrate it unto the one that brought them out of Egypt, but they celebrated it unto a golden calf, saying it was the one that brought them out of Egypt, and this is why YHWH got mad at them and rebuked them for the worship of the calf but not for the day/feast itself. Exodus 32:4.

I had an e-mail discussion with another lunar Sabbatarian who believes in lunar Sabbaths but not the 50 days after the seventh Sabbath Pentecost. Another Brother, Abraham, defend my position and wrote the following.

"Brother David,

You can check Koehler and Baumgartner yourself. AD can be a conjunction.

Are Koehler and Baumgartner not scholars?

On that point, what are your credentials as a scholar? Do you have a degree?"

Abraham

The e-mail also goes on to say,

"The Hebrew word AD can have meanings that support a 50-day count AFTER seven weeks. I use the Koehler and Baumgartner lexicon. The following expressions in all capital letters come from their lexicon.

LATER IN THE FUTURE, count fifty days (AD has a future tense.)

AND then count fifty days (AD can be a conjunction.)

JUST BEFORE counting fifty days, count seven weeks"

Notice the above scholars along with Bullinger, and Ferra Fenton, whom I will quote shortly, understood that Leviticus 23:16 could be understood as the children of Israel understood it in Exodus 32:5, and that is to number 50 days AFTER the seventh Sabbath complete.

Again, Ferrar Fenton in The Ferrar Fenton Bible actually reads this way, it Says,

"You shall also count for yourselves from the day after the Sabbath that you bring the wave sheaf, seven Sabbaths. They must be complete. **Then after the seventh Sabbath, you shall count fifty days**, when you shall present a new offering to the EVERY LIVING" Leviticus 23:15-16

Someone might ask who is Fenton?

The following is from a web site on Fenton. "The *Holy Bible in Modern English,* commonly known as the **Ferrar Fenton Bible**, was one of the earliest translations of the Bible into modern English.

Work on the translation began in 1853 by a London businessman called Ferrar Fenton (1832–1920)...... The translation is noted for a rearranging of the books of the Bible into what the author believed was the correct chronological order. In the Old Testament, this order follows that of the Hebrew Bible. The name of Elohim was translated throughout the Old Testament as "The Ever-Living". The Bible is described as **"translated into English direct from the original Hebrew, Chaldee, and Greek languages."** For his translation of the Book of Job which appeared in 1898, Fenton was assisted by Henrik Borgström. This was "rendered into the same meter as the original Hebrew, word by word and line by line".

I do not say that Mr. Fenton was perfect, but he is a scholar who is in harmony with the other scholars on this verse and makes it very clear that the 50 days are numbered **AFTER** the seventh Sabbath and that is exactly how the children of Israel understood it according to Exodus 32:5.

Again, my Bullinger Lexicon gives the definition of the word until and says,

"until, as long as, marking the continuance of an ACTION up to the time of ANOTHER "action". Here, followed by the Gen., until, unto, marking the terminus ad quem, and spoken both of time and place."

This is how I understood the words before I even seen any of these definitions. You have an ACTION of COUNTING seven Sabbaths, even UNTO or up until the morrow AFTER the seventh Sabbath and then that action stops and you have ANOTHER action of NUMBERING 50 days, NOT one day; and then ye shall offer a new meat offering unto YHWH.

If there was only ONE action of numbering, as the traditional Pentecost keepers believe, and that one action of numbering was from the wave sheaf, then two different Hebrew word for COUNT and NUMBER would not have been used and the Scripture would read to number 50 days from the wave sheaf and then offer the new meat offering instead of numbering 50 days after the seventh Sabbath and then offer the new meat offering. But this is not the case because there are TWO actions, the first action is to COUNT seven Sabbaths and the second action is to NUMBER 50 days, NOT one day. There is a difference between count and number. They are two different Hebrew words but have the same number in the Strong's concordance. See chapter on count and number.

Even if the morrow after the seventh Sabbath was included in the first count for the seven Sabbaths, which would make the seven Sabbaths inexact, it still teaches to number 50 days AFTER the seventh Sabbath because the Hebrew word **shall is ALWAYS future tense.** Shall number is future tense and besides that, even unto the morrow or up until the morrow after the seventh Sabbath complete is 49 days NOT 50 because the morrow is not included in the count. Fenton must have understood this in his translation.

The word "shall" is ALWAYS future tense and this goes along with the above. Shall ye number 50 days, in Leviticus 23:16, is future tense but the fact of the matter is, even unto the morrow after the seventh Sabbath complete, is 49 days NOT 50 days.

The Hebrew word "until" means up until a certain point but not including that point, and it would bring you to the BEGINNING of the morrow after the seventh Sabbath which is 49 days counted, not 50.

I say the verse should be understood to count seven Sabbaths up until the morrow after the seventh Sabbath, and then INCLUDING the morrow after the seventh Sabbath number 50 days and then offer a new meat offering. Either way you want to look at it, the children of Israel understood it to be 50 days after the seventh Sabbath and that is what really counts. Exodus 32:5

 Remember there is a difference between "counting" and "numbering".

Even though Strong's concordance uses the same number for both words, they are TWO different words in the Hebrew Interlinear. There is also a difference between weeks and days and the instructions were to COUNT the weeks/Sabbaths and then NUMBER the 50 days, not number one more day, but 50.

The above scholars and translations are in Harmony with the Chag that Aaron and the children of Israel proclaimed in Exodus 32:5 which was 50 days AFTER the seventh lunar Sabbath, Leviticus 23:16 and this brings you to the summer wheat harvest. These translations are also in harmony with the new wine that was in the presses on the day of Pentecost in the second chapter of the book of Acts and as the prophet Joel prophesied in the second chapter of Joel etc. there are no ripe grapes in the third month, and neither is there a Chag mentioned in the third month for the traditional third month Pentecost.

These scholars and these translations are also in harmony with the Pentecost **summer** wheat harvest in the FOURTH MONTH, mentioned by our Saviour in John 4:35, where it teaches there are four months then cometh the harvest, not 6 or seven months and then come with the harvest, as is the case with Winter wheat.

These scholars and translations are also in harmony with the many other things that I have mentioned and will mention in this search for the true Pentecost.

After all is said and done it really doesn't matter how the scholars understood and interpret the Hebrew word "until" in Leviticus 23:16 but what does matter is how the inspired Word of YHWH teaches how the children of Israel understood and interpreted it and according to Exodus 32:5 and Joel chapter 2 etc., it was 50 days after the seventh Sabbath and this is also confirmed in nature itself, concerning the grapes and the harvest.

Chapter 11

Day Another argument

Some say Pentecost is 50 days from the wave sheaf because the Hebrew word for "day" in Lev-23:16 is singular in Hebrew. While it is true that day is singular when it says "shall ye number fifty days", the plural is understood because 50 is plural.

Some don't understand that in MANY places in Scripture the Hebrew word for day is used in the singular form but is understood as plural, depending on how it is used in the sentence.

When the singular form for day comes after a number more than one, it is always understood as plural. Example, the flood was on the earth 40 days, but the Hebrew uses the singular form of the word DAY instead of the plural form, but it is understood that the flood was upon the earth 40 days/plural, not 40 day/singular. It was used this way 797 times where it is understood as plural but is written as singular, but because of the verse it is in shows it should be understood as plural.

The number 50 is plural and the phrase, shall you number 50 day/days should be understood as plural even though the singular is used, same as the 40 days/day the flood was upon the Earth.

We have many examples where the singular form of the Hebrew word for day appears in a verse but is understood in the plural sense, which kills this whole argument. Here are a few examples,

Examples,

In the Hebrew Interlunar by J.P. Green, Sr. shows the following Hebrew word for "day" in the singular but from the verse we see it is understood as plural.

Ge 7:4 "For yet seven days Mwy, and I will cause it to rain upon the earth forty days Mwy and forty nights;"

Notice the singular Hebrew word for day is preceded by the number 40 and therefore understood as plural even though the Hebrew word for day is singular in this verse, same as Lev-23:16, where it says number 50 days.

Ge 7:12 And the rain was upon the earth forty days Mwy and forty nights.

It is clear from this verse that there were 40 days and 40 nights/plural but the Hebrew word for day is singular, same as Leviticus 23:16 where it says number 50 days.

Ge 7:13 In the selfsame **day** Mwy entered Noah, and Shem.... into the ark.

Note the word "day" in verse 13 is plural in J.P. Green Interlinear but should be understood as singular, right opposite. This conclusively proves that it depends on how the word appears in the verse as to whether it is understood as singular or plural which kills the singular argument of Lev-23:16 made by some traditional Pentecost proponents.

Ge 7:17 "And the flood was forty days upon the earth; and the waters increased"

Again! Forty "day" (singular) is understood as plural even though the singular form of the word is used in Hebrew. There are many more, but I will skip down to chapter 50,

Ge 50:3 And forty days were fulfilled for him; for so are fulfilled the days of those which are embalmed: and the Egyptians mourned for him threescore and ten days.

Day is used in the Hebrew singular 3 times in this one verse but is understood in the plural and no one can intelligently argue that day is understood as plural in this verse.

Ex 24:18 "And Moses went into the midst of the cloud, and gat him up into the mount: and Moses was in the mount forty days and forty nights".

We have the same thing again here in this verse, the Hebrew word for day is singular but the plural is understood.

Nu 13:25 And they returned from searching of the land after forty days.

Same thing again, day is singular in Hebrew, but the translators translated it as plural because that is the way it should be understood and the same is true with Leviticus 23:16.

All of these and many many more, too numerous to mention, has the singular form of the Hebrew word for day that is assuredly talking about plural days which prove that just because the Hebrew singular form of the word day is used, does not mean it is understood as singular. This happened 797 times, too many times to quote all but my point is that Lev-23:16 is one of the 797 times and to say this disproves the later Pentecost is not wise.

Another thing some people do not understand is the Hebrew word "day" denotes a space of time and not just a 24hr day or days. The Hebrew word Yom /day can mean a month week or even a year. Example,

Da 10:2 In those days I Daniel was mourning three FULL weeks.

Notice the Hebrew word for FULL is "Yom".

Da 10:3 I ate no pleasant bread, neither came flesh nor wine in my mouth, neither did I anoint myself at all, till three WHOLE weeks were fulfilled.

Here again the word WHOLE is Yom.

Le 25:29 And if a man sell a dwelling house in a walled city, then he may redeem it within a whole year after it is sold; *within* a full YEAR may he redeem it.

Here the word for YEAR is Yom. It is a year of days, not a revolution year/equinox.

1Sa 27:7 And the time that David dwelt in the country of the Philistines was a full year and four months.

Again, YEAR is the Hebrew word Yom.

I could go on and on, but my point is that just because the Hebrew word "day" is singular in Lev-23:16, does not prove counting 50 days from the wave sheaf as some suggest and neither does it disprove numbering 50 days after the seventh Sabbath.

Chapter 12

THE COUNT

Mountainous is the evidence we have compiled thus far in favor of a fourth month Pentecost and in stark contrast to the current traditional count.

The path this evidence has inevitably led us to is the interpretation of the primary Pentecost command found in Leviticus 23:15-16:

*15And ye shall count unto **you from the morrow after the Sabbath**, from the day that ye brought the sheaf of the wave offering; **seven Sabbaths shall be <u>complete</u>**: 16Even <u>unto the morrow **after**</u> the seventh Sabbath shall ye **number fifty days;** and ye shall offer a new meat offering unto YHWH.*

The daunting task for the traditional Pentecost Proponents is to harmonize the third month theology with the conflicting scriptural fourth month revelation of proof.

This accomplishment is more simplistic than it may appear. One key to understanding the correct view of Leviticus 23:15-16 is to allow the extremely supportive information presented to open your mind to the possibility of another way of counting.

The breakdown of this passage reveals seven essential elements that can be dissected in order to unveil the intended thought of the author:

* Count

* Morrow after "the Sabbath"

* Wave sheaf

* Seven Sabbaths complete

* Morrow "after" seventh Sabbaths

* Number

* New meat offering

Three of these seven aspects have been extensively addressed in other chapters. For instance;

* We understand conclusively that the 15th day of Abib is the Sabbath every year. Therefore the "morrow after the Sabbath" must be the 16th day.

* We know that the "wave' sheaf" brought on the 16th day is of the barley harvest from the crop already in the land when Israel arrived.

* In conjunction, we know that the *"new meat offering"* is from the harvest that Israel would plant from *"their labors, which they had sown"*, which is the **summer** wheat harvest that is more than 50 days from Abib 16 because wheat that "they" sowed will not produce in 50 days!

This only leaves us to discern the four remaining components that need to correspond to what we know of the other three. We will begin with "counting" and "numbering". The command of Leviticus comprises two counts, not just one.

The following rendering is taken from the Strong's Exhaustive Concordance, 2004 Word Study Edition.

Chapter 13

Journey to the Mount and Count and Number;

H 5608; saphar; a primitive root; properly to *score* with a mark as a tally or record, i.e., (by implication) to *inscribe*, and also to *enumerate*; intensive to *recount*, i.e., *celebrate*. Used in many applications, "Saphar" is a verb meaning to number, recount, to relate, to declare.

It is used to signify the numbering or counting of objects (Ge 15:5; Ps 48:12, 13); and people, as in a census (1 Ch 21:2; 2 Ch 2:17). It also refers to a quantity that is too great to number (Ge 16:10; Jer 33:22). The number of steps as a sign of YHWH's care (Job 14:16; Mt 10:30).

The word also means to relate or to recount and used often to refer to the communication of important information and truths to those who have not heard them, especially to foreign nations (Ex 9:16; 1 Ch 16:24, Ps 96:3); or the children in Israel (Ps 73:15; 78:4,6; 79:13). The matter communicated included "dreams" (Ge 40:9; 41:8, 12; Jgs 7:13); and YHWH'S works (Ex 18:8; Ps 73:28; Jer 51:10). Even creation declares the glory and wisdom of YHWH (Job 12:8; 28:27; Ps 19:1,2).

Basically, what we see here are two ways of looking at the word. One is to "declare", and the other is to "number" something. The importance of this difference shines through in the duality of the instruction on how to determine the time of Pentecost AND in the fact that the word is rendered in TWO

DIFFERENT FORMS in the Hebrew.

COUNT - -- sjPx

NUMBER -- eyrPxj

The forms here connote the subtleties between "enumerate" and "numerate". When the intent is to "count" (enumerate), the idea is to name how many of something there are, not necessarily to arrange in an order or sequence. For example, if one is to "count" the men with mustaches, all we are doing is determining how many, the men are not in any particular order.

When the intent is to "number" (numerate), the idea is to name things in an order or sequence. For example, if one is to

"number" the men from oldest to youngest, we are establishing an order or sequence.

Consequently, when something is "declared", it is a form of "enumerating". The Sabbaths are "counted", i.e., "declared" or "enumerated", and the 50 days are "numbered", i.e., "numerated" in order and sequence. Now let's look at how this applies to the instruction in Leviticus.

First, all of the "Mowedim" or feast days of YHWH are reckoned by "declaration" as opposed to a "numbering". It is not necessary to "number" the days, months, and years because the heavenly luminaries "declare" them for us (Genesis 1:14).

The equal light and darkness "declares" the year, the New Moon "declares" the month, the biblical setting of the sun "declares" the end of one day and the beginning of a new one. The "weeks" are no different, they are "declared" by the ***phases*** of the moon. It is historically documented that the weeks were originally determined by the phases of the moon. Many if not most people know that the months were originally by the moon but fail to realize that the four phases of the moon were used for the weeks.

* The Universally Jewish Encyclopedia and another 100-year-old Jewish Encyclopedia by Funk & Wag, both record that ancient

Israel originally kept lunar weeks. See 1943 Universal Jewish Encyclopedia volume 10 page 482 edited by Isaac Landman under the article **"WEEK"**, written by Simon

Cohen, The Director of Research, and the 1943 Universal Jewish Encyclopedia volume 5 page 410 edited by Isaac

Landman under the article "HOLIDAYS", written by a well-respected Rabbi, Max

Joseph, for proof.

* Philo the Jew, which lived at the same time our Savior did, recorded that the weeks were by the moon and also Clement of Alexander. See Philo chapter. Ask for our free books Proof That the True Weekly Sabbaths or Determined by the Phases of the Moon.

* Other reference material and encyclopedia's report the origin of lunar-based weeks by human society.

The fact of historically and scripturally logical, lunar-based weeks, indicates the fact of a lunar based Sabbath by default. In the same way our current Roman based calendar system indicates a Roman week and therefore, a Roman based Sabbath. At the end of a Roman week, you have a Roman Sabbath and at the end of a Lunar week you have a Lunar Sabbath.

For a complete understanding of YHWH's calendar and the Sabbaths as they were originally reckoned by the phases of the moon, you may visit the website: lunarsabbath.info

Meanwhile, suffice it to say for now that the primary method of lunar Sabbath reckoning is six days of work, one day of rest through the month; the New Moon worship day is observed, then the work/rest scheduled resumes for the month. The new moon worship day is not counted in with the six working days according to YHWH in Ezekiel 46:1. This is repeated every month throughout the year.

The second aspect of the word "saphar" is to "number". A different form of the word is used, which specifically indicates a two-pronged instruction. The word **_shall number_** is *future tense* in Lev. 23:16. The count starts after the seventh Sabbath.

*16Even unto the morrow **after** the seventh Sabbath **shall** ye number fifty days; and ye shall offer a new meat offering unto YHWH.*

True Count to Pentecost

The following chart shows that if you count seven **lunar** Sabbaths complete (which do not include New Moon days when counting out the weeks, Ezekiel 46:1) unto the morrow "**after**" the seventh Sabbath and **then** number 50 days, it will be the exact same day that Aaron, YHWH'S high priest, proclaims a **Chag** to YHWH.

"1st Month"

1 2 3 4 5 6 7 *8th* [Sabbath]

9 10 11 12 13 *14th* [the Lamb slain between the evenings]

15th [Sabbath and **1st day** of feast of Unleavened Bread and day Houses **Passed over** in Egypt and thrust out of Rameses **Num-33:3**]

16th [is wave sheaf and "beginning" of count for the "7 Sabbaths" complete]

17 18 19 20 21 *22nd* [**1st** Sabbath]

23 24 25 26 27 28 *29th* [**2nd** Sabbath] 30

"2nd Month "

1 2 3 4 5 6 7 *8th* [**3rd** Sabbath]

9 10 11 12 13 14 *15th* [**4th** Sabbath]

16th [1st day of manna (Ex-16:1-29)]

17 18 19 20 21 *22nd* [**5th** Sabbath]

23 24 25 26 27 28 *29th* [**6th** Sabbath]

« 3rd Month»

1 2 3 4 5 6 7 *8th* [**7th** Sabbath complete]

9th [day is the "first day" "**AFTER**" 7th Sabbath and the 1st day of the SECOND count where you are to **NUMBER** 50 days and **then** bring a new meat offering to YHWH. **Lev-23:15-16**]

True Count to Pentecost

10th is 2nd day, 11/3rd, 12/4th, 13/5th, 14/6th, 15 [is Sabbath and 7th day of the count]

16/8th [day of the count to Pentecost and day they came to the Mount **(Ex-19:1-3)** see also The Book of **Jubilees Ch. 1:1** they were also told on 16th to be ready for **3rd** day **Ex-19:11**]

17/9th, **18**/10th [day of count and it was also the **3rd day when YHWH spoke to people (Ex-19:10-24)**]

19/11th [day of count and also **1st** day that Moses goes Into Mt. for 40 days and 40 nights. **Ex-24:4-18**]

20/12th [day of count and **2nd** day Moses in Mt.]

21/13th, 22 [Sabbath and 14th day of count]

23/15th, 24/16th, 25/17th, 26/18th, 27/19th, 28/20th 29**th** [Sabbath and 21st day of the count to Pentecost] a **30**-day month would make it the 22nd day of the count to Pentecost.

"4th Month"

1/23rd, 2/24th, 3/25th, 4/26th, 5/27th, 6/28th, 7/29th, **8th**/30th [Sabbath]

9/31st, 10th/32nd, 11/33rd, 12/34th, 13/345th, 14/36th, **15th** [Sabbath and 37th day of count to Pentecost]

16/38th, 17/39th, 18/40th, 19/41st, 20/42nd, 21/43rd, **22**/44th 9Sabbath]

23/45th, 24/46th, 25/47th, 26/48th, 27/49th, **28th**/50th.

The New Meat offering is brought on the **29th** Sabbath.

The beginning of the **29th** was the **40th** NIGHT of Moses' stay in the Mount and the **29th** morning is the day that the **Law** and tables of stone was ACTUALLY given to Moses (**Ex-31:18** and **Deut- 9:11**). This puts us exactly 102 days after the Passover, which is the same time Aarons declared the chag of Pentecost.

As YHWH promised in **Ex-24:12** which was «AFTER» the **50th** day was numbered. It was the day the Law was given, and the only way to commemorate this monumental event on the **same day** is to follow the instructions that were given by YHWH, not by the traditions of mankind.

You have seven weeks (six workdays plus a Sabbath which equals forty-nine days).

Then, you have fifty days from the morrow after the seventh Sabbath, a total of ninety-nine. That total plus three New moon days, worship days that are not counted as one of the six ordinary workdays or weekly Sabbaths totals 102 days.

One objection to the number of days in this count has to do with the meaning of Pentecost. Since Pentecost means "fifty", this provides proof positive to some as to the traditional third month count. However, the meaning of "fifty" is securely preserved in the count revealed above.

To count seven Sabbaths is part one of the instructions. In the tradition count the second part of the instruction would be to count "one" more day. Just remember "one" does not mean Pentecost, but fifty means Pentecost. The road to Pentecost is "50 days" after the seventh Sabbath, not "one" day.

Just think for a minute, you can have all this harmony by understanding only one scripture differently, and that is *"the morrow after the seventh Sabbath shall you number fifty days"* instead of numbering 50 days from the first Sabbath or wave sheaf. That isn't too much to give up for so much harmony, and if were not for tradition, it would be accepted right away.

It is amazing how people will follow some blind leaders who don't even believe in the son of YHWH, in contrast to what the scripture teaches. Remember the Jews are not scripture, the Baptist Church is not Scripture, and the Catholic Church is not scripture.

The Scripture is scripture, so stay with what it says and be saved, and not the tradition of men and be lost.

Paul said, *"After the way they call Heresy, so worship I the Mighty One of our Fathers."* Nothing can be found that goes against beginning the count of fifty days after the seventh Sabbath, except the tradition of men. Plenty of scriptures can be found to disprove counting from the first Sabbath.

In closing this chapter, we believe that just as sure as YHWH is restoring the SOUND of His true Name back to His people, which is pronounced Yuh Wuh, as in Hallelu Yuh, He is restoring His true Pentecost, and His true Sabbaths. For more on the True SOUND of the sacred name of God, click http://lunarsabbath.info/id60.html Or you can order the book from Amazon, True SOUND of The Sacred Name of God. I make no money; you just pay for printing. I charge nothing, not because it is worthless, but because it is priceless.

Just like the first recorded Pentecost on the day the law was given to them written in stone, there were about three thousand souls destroyed. (Ex. 32:28) In addition, when the law was written in their hearts on Pentecost years later, they were about three thousand souls saved (Acts 2:41).

We certainly know that this chapter does not begin to answer all questions pertaining to this very important subject so we reserve the right to add to or change as the eyes of our understanding are opened further by the Heavenly Father YHWH, pronounced Yuh Wuh, and if we have to make any changes for the purpose of correction, we will do so as He leads us, as all honest truth seekers should do.

When we become perfect, we will not have to change any more. We will be perfect as He is perfect, and He changes not. Feel free to make copies in part or all and share with others.

What we have seen in Scripture, observed in the nature, and science of astronomy, and agriculture, and witnessed in the pages of history, all harmoniously culminate to this count.

The method promoted in *any other* system or doctrine or by another count simply will not meet the requirements of all these elements. One aspect will suffer in order accommodate another. The calculation above is the only reckoning method that allows all YHWH'S true Pentecost feast/chag commandments to come to life. We serve a living Elohim by His living Word.

The Scripture teaches that nature "itself" teaches certain things and nature does not lie. And when there are two interpretations of a Scripture as is the case with Leviticus 23:16, and one of the interpretations will harmonize with what nature teaches, but the other contrary to what nature teaches and is mathematically impossible, which of the two interpretations of the Scriptures should you choose?

Do you believe the Scripture would actually contradict something that is taught in nature or go against a mathematical certainty?

Example: nature teaches that grapes are ripe in the summer but what if you had a Scripture with two possible interpretations, one that would harmonize the grapes being ripe in the **summer** but the other interpretation would have to have the grapes ripening in the **springtime** which is agriculturally impossible, would you choose to hold to your traditional interpretation of the Scripture or switch to the one that harmonizes with nature?

If you're interpretation of Scripture forces you to have to believe that wheat is ripe in 50 days when nature itself teaches that this is agriculturally impossible, would you change to the other interpretation of the Scripture even though it goes against your tradition that you were taught i.e., deny these fact in order to hold your tradition?

The Scripture will not go against FACTS found in Nature or Math. That's all I got to say about that. Truth has no fear of open debate.

Truth is freedom. He said we shall know the truth and the truth will make us free. Lies will keep you in bondage.

In the next chapters we will continue to confirm this marvelous re-emergence of truth in the life of Moses and the Israelite people, the Apostle Paul, Nehemi, Ezra, the prophet Joel and many others including the ancient Celtic peoples in history.

By their not being one single Scripture from Genesis to Revelations of a wheat harvest or harvest of any kind, in the third month, ought to be worth something in our search for truth. Also, the fact that Aaron proclaimed a feast/chag in the fourth month which can be harmonized with so many Scriptures including Leviticus 23:16 should be worth something also.

We can argue Leviticus 23:16 until Judgment Day or we can move on and see how Moses and the children of Israel understood it, after all, they spoke the language and were there.

If the Pentecost wheat was Winter wheat that is harvested in the spring and takes seventh month to harvest instead of four months to harvest as our Saviour said, it would have been destroyed by the hail because the Scripture says it distorted every green herb and the grasses of the field but with the summer Pentecost wheat that is planted in the first month and harvested in the fourth month, would have still been under the ground or as the King James says had not grown up/ still in darkness, would not have been hurt by the hail.

You cannot even find a conclusive Winter wheat harvest in Scripture, but you can find the summer wheat harvest in Scripture.

Again, I say we move past the two interpretations of Leviticus 23:16 and see how it was understood by

Moses and the children of Israel who were there and eyewitnesses. Is that fair enough that we move on and see how they understood it and let Scripture interpret Scripture?

Chapter 14

Days Travelling to the Mount

The following Scriptures prove that it is **MATHEMATICALLY IMPOSSIBLE** for the children of Israel to have reached Sinai in time for the traditional third month Pentecost.

The children of Israel departed from Ramseys on the 15th day of the FIRST month, Numbers 33:3, and the Almighty spoke to them in the wilderness of Sin on the 15th day of the SECOND month, Exodus 16:1. Total of 30 days

Judging from my map of the children of Israel's journey from Ramseys to the Wilderness of Sin which is approximately 150 mi. and when we do the math, we find approximately 150 mi. being traveled in 30 days and by dividing 30 into 150 we see that they had averaged **5 mi. per day**.

They stayed in the camp at the wilderness of Sin for at least seven days which brings us to a total of **37 days** toward the traditional 50-day count to Pentecost.

My Map shows it is approximately **220 mi. from Ramseys to Riphidim which leaves 70 more miles across the wilderness of Sin to Riphidim. If it took 30 days for them to cover the 150 mi. from Ramseys to the Wilderness of Sin, we can safely conclude that it took another 14 days to travel 70 mi. through the wilderness of Sin to Riphidim, using the 5mi. per day totaling 51 days** counting the 7 day stay gathering manna.

When they camped at Riphidim there was no water there and the children of Israel murmured because after 14 days their water was gone and they were dying of thirst, so Moses strikes the rock etc. and afterwards they **were attacked** by Amalek and Moses told Joshua to go out **TO MORROW and fight against Amalek Exodus 17:8 which would add another day to the 51 days, totaling 52 days** and on the morrow the

battle lasted all day until the going down of the sun, verse 12, which would be going into the <u>53rd day</u>.

On day 53, Moses was told to write a book and he also built an altar to the Almighty, verse 14 and 15.

Even if they left Riphidim on <u>day 54</u> writing a book and building an altar then traveled approximately <u>10mi.</u> to the mount, it would be at least <u>day 55</u> when they reached the mount and if the Almighty spoke the 10 commandments to them <u>three days</u> later, which would be a total of <u>58 days</u> from Ramseys, too late for the traditional Pentecost. What day do you keep Pentecost on?

This timeline is being very generous, and it shows they could not have reached the mount in the third month for the traditional Pentecost. Someone might question the 5 mi. per day average but a grown man alone can travel 15 to 20 mi. per day but when we consider women and children moving all their belongings alone with the gold and different treasures from Egypt, I believe we can safely assume that the children and women could not travel the same distance in a day as a grown man, maybe one half the distance which would be seven to 10 mi. per day. On top of this, herding the animals, sheep, goats, and cattle, not to mention any poultry etc. at any rate around 5 mi. per day seems reasonable for such a great multitude traveling in the wilderness, carrying everything they have, headed for a new land. **And it does not really matter whether it seems reasonable to someone or not because according to the pinpointed number of days, and the distance traveled, 5 mi. per day was the average, this is an absolute.**

All someone has to do is realize that ancient Israel and Israel today sows spring wheat in the spring and reaps it in the summer and this is the true Pentecost wheat which is 50 days after the seventh Sabbath complete according to Leviticus 23:16 NOT the Winter wheat that is sown in the winner and reaped in the spring after Barley harvest. see http://lunarsabbath.info/_wsn/page4.html

Brother Arnold http://lunarsabbath.info/index.html

Exodus 19:1-2 KJV says,

[1] "In the "third month", when the children of Israel were gone forth out of the land of Egypt, the "same day" (15th or16th) came they into the wilderness of Sinai. [2] For they were departed from Rephidim, and were come to the desert of Sinai, and had pitched in the wilderness; and there Israel camped before the mount."

The "same day", in Exodus 19:1, is referring to the "same day" that they went forth out of the land of Egypt, the Book of Jubilees says it was the 16th day of the 3rd month that they came to the mount, which I believe is correct because they were driven from Ramses on the 15th, and it would take them another day to reach the border of Egypt and go out of the land, on the 16th.

Although the law was spoken to Moses before it was given to him, it was not actually given to him until the "end" of the 40 days and 40 nights in the mount, **Deuteronomy 9:11 and Exodus 31:18**, and when we add the 54 days getting to the mount, with the 7 days Moses was in the mount, and to the end of the 40 days and forty nights, when the law was actually given, it comes to 101 days, which is more in line with counting 50 days after the seventh Sabbath than 50 days after the wave sheaf.

Deuteronomy 9:11 KJV says,

[11] "And it came to pass at the "end" of forty days and forty nights, that the LORD gave me the two tables of stone, even the tables of the covenant."

Exodus 31:18 KJVS

[18] "And he gave unto Moses, when he had made an "end" of communing with him upon mount Sinai, two tables of testimony, tables of stone, written with the finger of God."

I don't know where my notes on this is, and I don't feel like refiguring it, so I am writing this from memory and it may not be exact, but you can see my point of a later Pentecost.

Chapter 15

The Prophet Ezra observed Pentecost 50 days after the seventh Sabbath on the first day of the fifth month.

Ezra observed Pentecost and visited Jerusalem according to the Law of YHWH that was in his hand and it was on the new moon of the fifth month which can happen with the true Pentecost that is 50 days after the seventh Sabbath but not with 50 days after the wave sheaf.

The Septuagint makes it crystal clear that Ezra and the males went up to Jerusalem for Pentecost as the law teaches. I will read it first and then the Hebrew translation of the text which teaches the same thing. The Septuagint says, in Ezra 7:14, "one has been sent from the king and the seven counselors to **"visit"** Judea and Jerusalem, "**according to the law of YHWH <u>that is in thine hand.</u>**"

Notice: it was according to the law of YHWH that they were to visit Jerusalem, and it so happened that this was done 50 days AFTER the Seventh Sabbath.

Ezra visited Jerusalem on the first day of the fifth month. Ask yourself what Law of YHWH teaches to visit Jerusalem in the FIFTH month which is 50 days after the Seventh Sabbath not 50 days after the wave sheaf???

The law of YHWH that is in our hands today teaches there are only three times in the year that the males were commanded to appear before YHWH in Jerusalem and that is Unleavened Bread, Pentecost, and Tabernacles. We know that Tabernacles and Unleavened Bread cannot fall on the FIRST DAY OF THE FIFTH MONTH, but Pentecost can if you follow the instructions in Leviticus 23:16 and count 50 days AFTER the seventh Sabbath instead of 50 days after the wave sheaf. This so happened to be the day that Aaron and the children of Israel observed as a Chag in the wilderness, Exodus 32:5.

Unlike the other two feasts, that are fixed on a certain date of the moon, 15th, we have to count for Pentecost. With lunar sabbaths, it can fall on the day of the new moon, or the sabbath, or next to the sabbath, as Josephus recorded happened, and therefore we have to count to Pentecost.

The Septuagint makes this very clear about Ezra going up to Jerusalem, but the King James is not so clear but when you understand the Hebrew words it will harmonize with the Septuagint perfectly, it reads,

Ezr 7:14 Forasmuch as thou art sent of the king, and of his seven counsellers, to **inquire** concerning Judah and Jerusalem, according to the law of thy God which *is* in thine hand;

This will harmonize with the Septuagint when we understand that the Hebrew word "**inquire**" can be understood as "search or seek out" and then it would read **to search or seek out Jerusalem** according to the law that is in thine hand. This is comparable with the Septuagint which says **"visit"** Judea and Jerusalem, **"according to the law** of YHWH **that is in thine hand."** and of course this was done on the first day of the fifth month which is in harmony with 50 days AFTER the Seventh Sabbath in Leviticus 23:16 and was the same day that Aaron calls a Chag. Here's the Hebrew word for **"inquire"**,

Strong's Hebrew Dictionary 1240. b@qar (Aramaic) rqb b@qar (Aramaic) *bek-ar'*

(Aramaic) corresponding to 1239: --inquire, **make search**.

Notice this Hebrew word corresponds to 1239. baqar which means to "search or seek out".
"rqb baqar *baw-kar*
a primitive root; properly, to plough, or (generally) **break forth**, i.e. (figuratively) to inspect, admire, care for, consider: --(make) inquire (-ry), (make) **search, seek out**."

True Count to Pentecost

In light of all the other Scriptures I do not believe this is no coincidence concerning the date that Ezra and the males went up to Jerusalem according to the law.

The Scripture teaches a feast in the springtime/ Unleavened Bread, a feast in the summertime/ Pentecost, and a feast in the fall/Tabernacles. They are equally spaced out and looks like this,
1 - - 4 - - 7, not like this, 1 – 3 - - - 7
there is a feast in the spring, one in the summer, and another in the fall. The traditional Pentecost keepers have TWO feasts in the spring, NONE in the summer, and one in the fall not allowing as much time after returning from Passover before it is time to go right back up to Jerusalem again for Pentecost. The true count to Pentecost spaces it out more evenly which is less of a strain on the travelers.

Remember that Ezra found a book of the law, telling them to go to Jerusalem for Pentecost, so Ezra and the **males** went up for the commanded feast at the commanded time to appear before YHWH according to the law that was in his hand, and it was at the beginning of the fifth month which is the firstfruits of the summer wheat harvest.

An interesting note is that to this very day the Anglo-Saxons, which are descendants of Ancient Israel, observe, August 1, as the FIRST FRUITS OF THE WHEAT HARVEST. Look up "Lammas" in about any dictionary, and you will see that it means "loaf mass" and tells how that loaves of the "FIRSTFRUITS " of the WHEAT harvest were offered on the altar at this time etc. which I will deal with in another chapter, but we will now look at the King James Version and other translations of Ezra 7th chapter.

Ezr 7:6 This Ezra went up from Babylon; and he *was* a **ready scribe** in the **law** of Moses, which YHWH Elohim of Israel had given: and the king granted him all his request, according to the hand of YHWH his Elohim upon him. **Ezr 7:7** And there went up *some* of the children of Israel, and of the priests, and the Levites, and the singers, and the porters, and the Nethinim's, unto Jerusalem, in the seventh year of Artaxerxes the king. **Ezr 7:8** And he came to Jerusalem in the **fifth month**, which *was* in the seventh year of the king. **Ezr 7:9** For upon the first day of the first month began he to go up from Babylon, and on the "**FIRST DAY** " of the **"FIFTH " month** came he to Jerusalem, according to the good hand of his Elohim upon him."

Notice: this fifth month would be at the time that Aaron and the children of Israel proclaimed a Chag/ feast to YHWH, Exodus 32:5 and the time of the summer wheat harvest which is 50 days AFTER the seventh Sabbath, according to the law that is in my hand and your hand, Leviticus 23:16. The grapes also will be ripe in time for the new wine as the prophet Joel prophesied and fulfilled In the 2nd Chapter of Acts. Continuing on,

Ezr 7:10 **For Ezra had prepared his heart to seek the law of YHWH**, and **to do it,** and **to teach in Israel statutes and judgments**.

Ezr 7:13 I make a decree, that all they of the people of Israel, and *of* his priests and Levites, in my realm, which are minded of their own freewill to go up to Jerusalem, go with thee. **Ezr 7:14** Forasmuch as thou art sent of the king, and of his seven counsellers, **to inquire concerning Judah and Jerusalem, according to the law of thy Elohim which *is* in thine hand;** **Ezr 7:15** And to carry the silver and gold, which the king and his counsellers have freely offered unto the Elohim of Israel, whose habitation *is* in Jerusalem, … **Ezr 7:21** And I, *even* I Artaxerxes the king, do make a decree to all the treasurers which *are* beyond the river, that whatsoever Ezra the priest, the scribe of the law of the Elohim of heaven, shall require of you, it be done speedily, **Ezr 7:22** Unto an hundred talents of silver, and to an **hundred measures of wheat,** and to an **hundred baths of wine**, and to an hundred baths of oil, and **salt** without prescribing *how much*. **Ezr 7:23** Whatsoever is **commanded** by the Elohim of heaven, let it be diligently done for the house of the Elohim of heaven: **for why should there be wrath against the realm of the king and his sons?"**

Again**,** Pentecost is one of the three major feasts/Chags where all the MALES were to appear before YHWH. Notice how chapter 8 stresses MALES going up to Jerusalem according to the law,

Ezr 8:1 These *are* now the chief of their fathers, and *this is* the genealogy of them that went up with me from Babylon, in the reign of Artaxerxes the king. **Ezr 8:2** Of the **SONS** of Phinehas; Gershom: of the **SONS** of Ithamar; Daniel: of the **SONS** of David; Hattush. **Ezr 8:3** Of the **SONS** of Shechaniah, of the **SONS** of Pharosh; Zechariah: and with him were reckoned by genealogy of the **MALES an hundred and**

fifty. **Ezr 8:4** Of the **sons** of Pahathmoab; Elihoenai the **son** of Zerahiah, and with him two hundred **MALES**. **Ezr 8:5** Of the **sons** of Shechaniah; the son of Jahaziel, and with him **three hundred MALES**. **Ezr 8:6** Of the **sons** also of Adin; Ebed the **son** of Jonathan, and with him **fifty MALES**. **Ezr 8:7** And of the **sons** of Elam; Jeshaiah the son of Athaliah, and with him **seventy MALES**. **Ezr 8:8** And of the **sons** of Shephatiah; Zebadiah the **son** of Michael, and with him **fourscore MALES**. **Ezr 8:9** Of the **sons** of Joab; Obadiah the **son** of Jehiel, and with him **two hundred and eighteen MALES**. **Ezr 8:10** And of the **sons** of Shelomith; the **son** of Josiphiah, and with him an **hundred and threescore MALES**. **Ezr 8:11** And of the **sons** of Bebai; Zechariah the **son** of Bebai, and with him **twenty and eight MALES**. **Ezr 8:12** And of the **sons** of Azgad; Johanan the **son** of Hakkatan, and with him an **hundred and ten MALES**. **Ezr 8:13** And of the last **sons** of Adonikam, whose names *are* these, Eliphelet, Jeiel, and Shemaiah, and with them **threescore MALES**. **Ezr 8:14** Of the **sons** also of Bigvai; Uthai, and Zabbud, and with them **seventy MALES**....

Remember Pentecost is one of the 3 major Feasts where all the **MALES** were to appear before YHWH.

Notice also that the king made the statement "**for why should there be wrath against the realm of the king and his sons?**" It appears the king believed he should allow the **sons** of Israel to go up to Jerusalem and carry things the law required for Pentecost. It is no coincidence that the MALES were singled out in this chapter and remember this also was according to the law of YHWH that was in his hand. In other words, the MALES were to "**VISIT**" Jerusalem on Pentecost according to the law that was in his hand and according to the Septuagint.

We will now look at a few other translations, beginning with the new American Standard Bible.

Ezra 7 (New American Standard Bible)

9For on the first of the first month he began to go up from Babylon; and on the "**first of the fifth month**" he came to Jerusalem, because the good hand of his God was upon him.

10For Ezra had set his heart to study the law of YHWH and to "**practice it**", and (G)to teach His statutes and ordinances in Israel.

Notice Ezra not only had set his heart to studying the law but to **PRACTICE IT** by going up to Jerusalem at this time of year/first day of the 5th month.

Ezra 7 (New Living Translation)

8 Ezra arrived in Jerusalem in August[e] of that year. **9** He had arranged to leave Babylon on April 8, the first day of the new year,[f] and he arrived at Jerusalem on August 4,[g] for the gracious hand of his God was on him. **10** This was **because** Ezra had determined to study and "**OBEY THE LAW**" of YHWH and to teach those decrees and regulations to the people of Israel....

Notice Ezra had determined to OBEY THE LAW by going up to Jerusalem at this proper time. e. Ezra 7:8 Hebrew *in the fifth month.* This month in the ancient Hebrew lunar calendar occurred within the months of August and September 458 b.c. f. Ezra 7:9 Hebrew *on the first day of the first month,* of the ancient Hebrew lunar calendar. This day was April 8, 458 b.c.; also see note on 6:15. g. Ezra 7:9 Hebrew *on the first day of the fifth month,* of the ancient Hebrew lunar calendar. This day was August 4, 458 b.c.; also see note on 6:15.

True Count to Pentecost

Ezra 7 (Contemporary English Version)

11 Ezra was a priest and an expert in the laws and commands that YHWH had given to Israel. One day King Artaxerxes gave Ezra a letter which said:

12 Greetings from the great King Artaxerxes to Ezra the priest and expert in the teachings of the God of heaven.

13-14 Any of the people of Israel or their priests or Levites in my kingdom may go with you to Jerusalem if they want to. My seven advisors and I agree that you may go to Jerusalem and Judah to find out if [e] the laws of your God are being obeyed.

<u>Ezra 7:8</u> *fifth month*: Ab, the fifth month of the Hebrew calendar, from about **"mid-July to mid-August"**.

Notice Ezra was going up to Jerusalem to find out if the Laws of YHWH were being obeyed and at this time was 50 days AFTER the seventh Sabbath that Ezra arrived at Jerusalem, and this would be the proper time to see if they were observing the law or not.

It is also interesting that the Celtic people or ancient Israelite people observed Pentecost at the end of the fourth month or **FIRST DAY OF THE FIFTH MONTH** same day that Ezra visited Jerusalem according to the Law and it was a new moon day of the fifth month that he was checking to see if Israel was keeping the Law. The Anglo-Saxon (ancient Israelites) people still keep the first **FRUITS OF THE WHEAT HARVEST on August 1** even to this day and this is no coincidence. See Chapter on Lammas.

Neither is it a coincidence that the prophet planned the journey so as to arrive in Jerusalem to teach and observed the law at the exact time that the law and tables of stone were originally given to Moses which was at the END of the 40 days and 40 nights **(Ex-31:18)** and **(Deut-9:11)** which was on the very day that Aaron and the children of Israel proclaimed a Chag feast to YHWH **(Ex-32:5)** and it was 50 days AFTER the seventh Sabbath according to Leviticus 23:16 and NOT in the 3rd month.

The following shows Ezra going up to Jerusalem to **teach** the law at Jerusalem on the very same day the Law was given to Moses for to teach Israel at

Mt. Sinai/Pentecost and it was on the first day of the **fifth month**, the very same time frame that Israel proclaimed a feast/Chag to YHWH, Exodus 32:5.

King James version reads, Ezr 7:10 For Ezra had prepared his heart to seek the law of YHWH, and to do *it*, and to <u>teach</u> in Israel statutes and judgments.

9For on the first of the first month he began to go up from Babylon; and on the **first** of the **fifth** month he came to Jerusalem, (E)because the good hand of his God was upon him.

10For Ezra had set his heart to study the law of YHWH and to practice it, and (G)to **teach His statutes and ordinances in Israel**.

Ezra 7 (New American Standard Bible)

8 Ezra arrived in Jerusalem in **August**[e] of that year. **9** He had arranged to leave Babylon on April 8, the first day of the new year,[f] and he arrived at Jerusalem on August 4,[g] for the gracious hand of his God was on him. **10** This was **because** Ezra had determined to study and **obey the Law** of YHWH **and to teach those decrees and regulations to the people of Israel....**

Notice the law will be presented again! On the same date it was given to Israel years earlier, at the end of the 40 days and 40 nights of Moses stay in the mount. See Deuteronomy 9:11 and Exodus 31:18. This date can fall on the last day of the fourth month or the first day of the fifth month depending on when the new moon begins. Continuing on,

16 "Furthermore, you are to take any silver and gold that you may obtain from the province of Babylon, as well as the voluntary offerings of the people and the priests that are presented for the Temple of their God in Jerusalem. **17** These donations are to be used specifically for the purchase of bulls, rams, male lambs, and the **APPROPRIATE GRAIN OFFERINGS** and liquid offerings, all of which will be offered on the altar of the Temple of your God in Jerusalem.

Notice the APPROPRIATE GRAIN OFFERINGS were wheat. Pentecost is when the first fruits of the wheat is offered to YHWH in Jerusalem.

18 Any silver and gold that is left over may be used in whatever way you and your colleagues feel is the will of your God.

e. Ezra 7:8 Hebrew *in the **fifth month**.* This month in the ancient Hebrew lunar calendar occurred within the months of **August** and September 458 b.c.

f. Ezra 7:9 Hebrew *on the first day of the first month,* of the ancient Hebrew lunar calendar. This day was April 8, 458 b.c.; also see note on 6:15.

g. Ezra 7:9 Hebrew *on the FIRST DAY of the FIFTH MONTH,* of the ancient Hebrew lunar calendar. This day was August 4, 458 b.c.; also see note on 6:15.

Ezra 7 (New Living Translation)

Ezra 7 (Contemporary English Version)

11 Ezra was a priest and an expert in the laws and commands that YHWH had given to Israel. One day King Artaxerxes gave Ezra a letter which said:

12Greetings from the great King Artaxerxes to Ezra the priest and expert in the teachings of the God of heaven.

13-14 Any of the people of Israel or their priests or Levites in my kingdom may go with you to Jerusalem if they want to. My seven advisors and I agree that you may go to Jerusalem and Judah to **FIND OUT IF [e] THE LAWS OF YOUR GOD ARE BEING OBEYED**

Ezra 7:8 *fifth month*: Ab, the fifth month of the Hebrew calendar, from about **MID-JULY TO MID-AUGUST**

Again, I find it very interesting and no coincidence that Ezra went up to Jerusalem to deliver and **teach** the law of YHWH to Israel on the very same day that it was given to Moses at Mt. Sinai for to **TEACH** Israel. **The bottom line is that when Ezra and the males went up to Jerusalem it corresponds with the very day that the law was first given to Moses, and this is no coincidence.**

Ex 24:12 And YHWH said unto Moses, Come up to me into the mount, and be there: and I will give thee

tables of stone, and a law, and commandments **which I have written**; that thou mayest **TEACH** them.

The question is, when was the law that He had written given so that it could be taught?

The answer is it was given at the END of the 40 days and 40 nights which would be after numbering 50 days AFTER the Seventh Sabbath. Ex 31:18 "And he gave unto Moses, when he had made an **END of** communing with him upon mount Sinai, two **tables of** testimony, **tables of stone**, written with the finger **of** God. " That's plain enough and it corresponds with the day Ezra and the males went up to Jerusalem.

De 5:22 These words YHWH spake unto all your assembly in the mount out **of** the midst **of** the fire, **of** the cloud, and **of** the thick darkness, with a great voice: and he added no more. And he wrote **them in two tables of stone, and delivered them unto me.**

De 9:9 When I was gone up into the mount to receive the **tables of stone**, *even* the **tables of** the covenant which YHWH made with you, then I abode in the mount forty days and forty nights, I neither did eat bread nor drink water: **De 9:10** And YHWH **delivered unto me** two **tables of stone written with the finger of God**; and on them *was written* according to all the words, which YHWH spake with you in the mount out of the midst of the fire in the day of the assembly. **De 9:11** "And it came to pass at the **END** of forty days and forty nights, *that* **YHWH gave me the two tables of stone,** *even* **the tables of the covenant.**" And that's plain enough.

This was the law that he had written and was given at the end of the fourth month or the beginning of the fifth month which Israel claimed it to be a feast/Chag to YHWH, see Exodus 32:5.

What are the odds of Ezra giving and teaching the law many years later to Israel on the same day that it was first given to Moses?

Did YHWH have anything to do with the timing of the law being presented to Israel again, on the same day that he gave it to Moses to teach the people?

Again, what better time to go up to Jerusalem with all the **males** in chapter 8 and teach and do the law, at the time that the law was originally given to the children of Israel?

It was also in the exact same season/time that the judgment of YHWH allowed His House to be destroyed by Nebuchadnezzar king of Babylon and the vessels thereof taken away, but now they are being returned at the exact same time that they were taken away years earlier and this is no coincidence either. I might also note that judgment on this same House of YHWH was destroyed again at this very same time by Titus in A.D. 70. See Josephus.

"The Talmud the Steinsaltz Edition", Volume XIV Tractate Ta'anit Part II (1995 by Israel Institute for Talmudic Publications and Milta Books), pages 205-206. It says the following regarding the destruction of the Jewish Temple in Jerusalem-built by Solomon and destroyed by Nebuchadnezzar's army: Page 205: *"Then late on the day of the ninth, close to nightfall, they set the Temple on fire, and it continued to burn the entire next day, on the tenth."* Page 206: *"When the Temple was destroyed for the first time at the hands of Nebuzaradan [captain of the guard], that day was the **ninth** of Av, and it was the **day following Shabbat**,* *(lunar sabbath is on the 8th) and it was the year following the Sabbatical Year.... And similarly when the Temple was destroyed a second time at the hands of Titus, the destruction occurred on the very same day, on the **ninth** of Av."*

Josephus was an eyewitness as to the timing of the destruction of the Temple in A.D. 70 and the Scripture teaches that Nebuchadnezzar destroyed it in the FIFTH MONTH, here's what he wrote.

However, **one cannot but wonder** at the accuracy of this period thereto relating; for the **same month and day** were now observed, as I said before, wherein **the holy house was burnt** formerly by the Babylonians.

5. (144) And now it was that the king of Babylon sent Nebuzaradan, the general of his army, to Jerusalem, to pillage the temple; who had it also in command to burn it and the royal palace, and to lay the city even with the ground, and to transplant the people into Babylon. (145) Accordingly he came to Jerusalem, in the eleventh year of king Zedekiah, and pillaged the temple, and **CARRIED OUT THE VESSELS** of God, both gold and silver, and particularly that large

laver which Solomon dedicated, as also the pillars of brass, and their chapiters, with the golden tablets and the candlesticks: (146) and when he had carried these off, he set fire to the temple in **THE FIFTH MONTH, FIRST DAY OF THE MONTH,** in the eleventh year of the reign of Zedekiah, and in the eighteenth year of Nebuchadnezzar; he also burnt the palace, and overthrew the city.

Notice the judgment of them breaking the law happened around Pentecost at the time the law was first given to Moses.

BOOK 10 CHAPTER 8 THE ANTIQUITES OF THE JEWS (131- 46)

CHAPTER 9

…1. (155) Now the general of the army, Nebuzaradan, when he had carried the people of the Jews into captivity, left the poor, and those that had deserted, in the country; and made one, whose name was Gedaliah, the son of Ahikam, a person of a noble family, their governor; which Gedaliah was of a gentle and righteous disposition. (156) He also commanded them that they should cultivate the ground, and pay an appointed tribute to the king. He also took Jeremiah the prophet out of prison, and would have persuaded him to go along with him to Babylon, ...2. (159) When Nebuzaradan had done thus, he made haste to Babylon; but as to those that fled away during the siege of Jerusalem, and had been scattered over the country, when they heard that the Babylonians were gone away, and had left a remnant in the land of Jerusalem, and those such as were to cultivate the same, they came together from all parts to Gedaliah to Mispah. (160) ...

BOOK 10 CHAPTER 8 THE ANTIQUITES OF THE JEWS (131- 159) **Jer 40:9** And Gedaliah the son of Ahikam the son of Shaphan sware unto them and to their men, saying, Fear not to serve the Chaldeans: dwell in the land, and serve the king of Babylon, and it shall be well with you. **Jer 40:10** As for me, behold, I will dwell at Mizpah to serve the Chaldeans, which will come unto us: but ye, **gather ye wine, and summer fruits**, and oil, and put *them* in your vessels, and dwell in your cities that ye have taken. **Jer 40:11** Likewise when all the Jews that *were* in Moab, and among the Ammonites, and in Edom, and that *were* in all the countries, heard that the king of Babylon had left a remnant of Judah, and that he had set over them Gedaliah the son of Ahikam the son of Shaphan; **Jer 40:12** Even all the Jews returned out of all places whither they were driven, and came to the land of Judah, to Gedaliah, unto Mizpah, and gathered **wine and summer fruits** very much.

Strong's Hebrew Dictionary
7019. qayits
Uyq qayits *kah'-yits*
from 6972; harvest (as the crop), whether the product (**grain or fruit**) or the (dry) season: --summer (fruit, house).

I believe the summer fruit is referring to the grain wheat harvest at end of the fourth month and beginning of the 5th month. It talked about a basket of summer fruit which is referring to wheat. At any rate it shows that Nebuchadnezzar destroyed the Temple in the summertime around 50 days after the seventh Sabbath, what we believe to be Pentecost. Brother Arnold www.lunarsabbath.info

8. (267) Now although anyone would justly lament the destruction of such a work as this was, since it was the

most admirable of all the works that we have seen or heard of, both for its curious structure and its magnitude, and also for the vast wealth bestowed upon it, as well as for the glorious reputation it had for its holiness; yet might such a one comfort himself with this thought, that it was fate that decreed it so to be, which is inevitable, both as to living creatures and as to works and places also. (268) However, **one cannot but wonder** at the accuracy of this period thereto relating; for the **same month and day** were now observed, as I said before, wherein **the holy house was burnt** formerly by the Babylonians. (269) Now the number of years that passed from its first foundation, which was laid by king Solomon, till this its destruction, which happened in the second year of the reign of Vespasian, are collected to be one thousand one hundred and thirty, besides seven months and fifteen days; (270) and from the second building of it, which was done by Haggai, in the second year of Cyrus the king, till its destruction under Vespasian, there were six hundred and thirty-nine years and forty-five days.   WARS OF THE JEWS BOOK 6 CHAPTEER 4 8. (267)   www.lunarsabbath.info

I have dealt with the Hebrew word "until" in Leviticus 23:16 in the first chapter and the Hebrew word for "count" in chapter 2 and Esther in chapter 3.

Chapter 16

WHAT ABOUT JOSEPHUS?

Don't Josephus say 50 days after the wave sheaf?

If all I had was Josephus and did not have all the conclusive evidence from scripture, Nature, and mathematic count etc., I could possibly justify counting from the wave sheaf for Pentecost.

Josephus does not say that the morrow after the seventh Sabbath is Pentecost. He says,

"When a week of weeks has passed over after this sacrifice (which weeks contain 49 days), on the fiftieth day, which is Pentecost, they bring to God "a" loaf, made of Wheat four..."

Response, notice it did not say ON THE NEXT DAY", "When a week of weeks has passed over after this sacrifice is Pentecost, they bring to God "a" loaf, made of Wheat four,.." but it says "ON THE 50TH DAY, which is Pentecost, they bring to God "a" loaf, made of Wheat four,..", i.e. on the FIFTIETH day AFTER a week of weeks has passed over.

We also believe that when a week of weeks has passed over after this sacrifice (which weeks contain 49 days), ON THE 50TH DAY, is Pentecost, i.e., on the "fiftieth" day "AFTER" the week of weeks has passed over. Leviticus 23:16 also teaches to number 50 days after seven Sabbath complete.

I can see how it can lean toward the traditional count and as I said, if this was all I had to go by, I could justify counting this way, but the above is not conclusive as to what he meant.

Notice also, the parentheses marks may have been added by the translator also because the translator said they bring to God **"a" loaf** and we all know that the Scripture stressed **"TWO" loaves.** This indicates the translator did not know much about the feasts and probably the traditional Pentecost influenced his interruption. The Ferr Fenton Bible actually says to number fifty days after the seventh Sabbath.

See my study on Philo who lived at the same time as our Saviour and how they kept Pentecost 50 days AFTER the seventh Sabbath complete. http://lunarsabbath.info/_wsn/page4.html

It is also possible that a week of weeks/49 days went by AFTER the 16th, a total of 50 days +50 more days.

Bible software called Accordance (a Mac program) and in the Hebrew bible module BHS-W4 there is a letter mem (מ) before the word "morrow", which when done like that does make the mem function as min, which means from

Deuteronomy 16:9-10 KJV, at first glance, also appears to contradict all the above conclusive evidence, but it only specifies when to begin to number the weeks, but does not go into any more details like Leviticus 23:16 does, which specifically says to number 50 days "after" the weak of weeks, or seven Sabbaths complete.

Deuteronomy says, [9] "Seven weeks shalt thou number unto thee: begin to number the seven weeks from such time as thou beginnest to put the sickle to the corn. [10] And thou shalt keep the feast of weeks unto the Lord thy God with a tribute of a freewill offering of thine hand, which thou shalt give unto the Lord thy God , according as the Lord thy God hath blessed thee:"

It tells us when to begin numbering the weeks and then keep Pentecost, but it does not say we keep it one day after, or 50 days after, and as I have shown that Pentecost means 50 not one, as Leviticus 23;16 says, and we are to keep Pentecost 50 days after the seventh sabbath, and we have all the approved examples in scripture showing that they kept Pentecost beyond the traditional 50 day count!

Me or no one can publish a more important book than the book I published on the True SOUND of the Name of God, which **conclusively proves** what the name of God is.

I do not charge anything for these books, not because they are worthless, but because they are priceless.

You can order from Amazon etc., you only pay the shipping and printing, which is not much, probably around $10.99, and if you can't afford it, get in touch with me, and I will take care of it for you.

If you know someone that is interested in keeping the true Pentecost, you can copy and paste the following and send it to them, and also give them the above article, thank you.

This amazing Pentecost discovery takes the guesswork out of how to count to Pentecost by conclusively proving from Scripture that the numbering of the 50 days begins on the morrow **AFTER** the seventh Sabbath complete, (**Leviticus 23:16**) instead of numbering from the wave sheaf. By doing this, it places Pentecost at the end of the **FOURTH** month instead of the beginning of the **THIRD** month.

Did you know that there is not even a THIRD month FEAST OF ANY KIND found in Scripture But there is in the fourth month? **WOW!**

Did you know that there is not even a conclusive WHEAT HARVEST or harvest of any kind in the THIRD month found in Scripture But there is in the fourth month? **WOW!**

Did you know that the **law** that was written with the finger of YHWH **was not given** to Moses until the **END OF THE FOURTH MONTH** which is 50 days AFTER the seventh Sabbath complete? **WOW!**

Did you know that Pentecost was one of the three major Pilgrim feasts that were called Chags in the Hebrew, where the children of Israel were commanded to travel up to Jerusalem each year and there is not even a Chag found in Scripture in the THIRD month but there is in the fourth month? **WOW!**

Did you know that there is Historical evidence of **Eyewitnesses** of people who lived at the same time of our Saviour and the Apostles, keeping Pentecost 50 days **AFTER** the seventh Sabbath complete? **WOW!**

Did you know that Acts chapters 20 and 21 shows that it is a **MATHEMATICAL CERTAINTY** that the Apostle Paul and thousands of believing Jews were keeping Pentecost **BEYOND** the traditional 50-day count? **WOW! WOW! WOW! See Scripture where the apostle Paul and thousands of believing Israelites observed Pentecost beyond the traditional 50-day count at Paul's Pentecost at http://lunarsabbath.us/id9.html**

Did you know that the Children of Israes kept Pentecost on the day that the Law was given, and they called it a Chag/Feast to YHWH, and it was exactly 50 days AFTER the 7th Sabbath? **WOW!**

Did you know that in light of all of this, along with the evidence that I am going to produce in this book, people will still keep their tradition of Pentecost in the THIRD month? **WOW!**

Did you know that what you do not know can DESTROY you? Hosea 4:6 says my people are DESTROYED for lack of knowledge. **WOW!**

Did you know that if we reject knowledge, that He will reject us? This is also found in Hosea 4:6 i.e., if we do not know something or have no knowledge of it, we are damned and if we reject the knowledge that is presented to us, we are damned. Did you know it is our duty to search out a matter, and if we do not well held accountable? **WOW!**

Having said that I will conclusively prove that Leviticus 23:16 should be understood the count to Pentecost is 50 days **AFTER** the seventh Sabbath complete, NOT 50 days after the wave sheaf!

Here are some of my notes on what the Scripture teaches is the true count to Pentecost which is 50 days **"after" the 7th Sabbath complete, <u>not</u> 50 days after the <u>wave sheaf</u> or 1st Sabbath.**

Lev-23:16 "Even unto the morrow <u>"after"</u> the seventh sabbath shall ye <u>number fifty days</u>; and ye shall offer a new meat offering unto YHWH" If you have Questions and wish to talk, my number is **(770) <u>483-8542</u>**

Below is an abundance of evidence from scripture and nature that conclusively proves a later Pentecost. **Go to http://lunarsabbath.us/id7.html** and you will see that even Nature Proves the 4th month Pentecost. Go to **http://lunarsabbath.us/id11.html** and see that it is **MATHEMATICALLY IMPOSSIBLE** for the children of Israel to have reached Mount Sinai in time for the traditional third month Pentecost.

Shalom

Remember, TRUTH is FREEDOM, he says you shall know the truth and the truth shall make you free, and once we know it, our lives will never be the same, we will be new creatures in the Messiah/MessYuh, Anointed Yuh. Hallelu Yuh.

Go to YouTube and type in Brother Arnold Bowen for videos

Brother Arnold Bowen at 3466 E. high tower Trail Conyers, GA 30012

Website http://lunarsabbath.info

Email lunarsabbath@aol.com and list other books

Radio station WWCR Live broadcast at http://wwcr.gsradio.net:3863/index.html?sid=1 Saturday 7:30 Pm Est and 4:00 Pm Thursday, click on listen

Also TUESDAY at 7:00 PM Est click on

http://wwcr.gsradio.net:3763/index.html?sid=1 And click on listen

Also Monday through Thursday at 10:15 Est on 3.215, and Saturday at 10:15, on 3.215

CPSIA information can be obtained
at www.ICGtesting.com
Printed in the USA
LVHW022233110921
697591LV00003B/9